If you get up one more time than you fall,
you will make it through.
Chinese proverb

Imprint
© Frederik Suter, 2017

book design: Renate Blaes
www.renateblaes.de

Frederik Suter

Suerte

or

the vicious circle
of happiness

autobiography

translated into English by

Caroline Clark-Maxwell
Fiona McAllister
Rosa Foyle
Fiona Garatt
and myself

Content

For my family
(and the English speaking world)

Bye then!

Right. It's all booked. Wow, this feels great. Three weeks in Catalonia. Alone. Too much? Am I expecting too much from myself? Admittedly, I am a little restricted due to being completely deaf and my balance is so bad at the moment that I am using a walker to get around.

It wasn't always this way. I used to be really sporty. I remember when I was seven years old the local football pitch would become almost like a second home to me for the best part of a decade. I would ring up my football friends, one by one, every day to ask whether they were coming out to play. Sometimes they couldn't come out, but it didn't matter, I'd just go along and meet new people or have a few shots at the goal. I'd go home at 6 o'clock and complain to my family about my bad luck - how often had I hit the posts or the bar? 22 times in 15 minutes. "Dammit! Unbelievable! Everything is against me!" The world had clearly conspired against me.

At home, along the side of the house towards the garden there was a wooden fence. I used to climb over it almost every day to go and play with the boy next door and sometimes I was allowed to stay for meals. He was football-mad too and we kicked a ball around wherever we could (his mother justifiably got annoyed if we kicked a ball around the house) and we played fierce matches in the garden. The score was never significant. Not for me, anyway. The fun that we had was all the more important.

His mother had noticed that something wasn't right with my hearing. I had noticed it too and it became more and more annoying.

Or, as always, at the bottom of the steps at the local supermarket, just a few meters away, my friend would call something to me that I simply couldn't catch and would I have to keep asking what he had said more and more often. During a summer holiday in France, I realised it was getting worse. I even showed my parents that I could hardly walk in a straight line any more. They thought I was joking. Unfortunately, this was also around the time that I discovered alcohol. In the evenings, as I made my way back in the dark, swaying back and forth and even once falling into the bushes at the camp site, alcohol was quickly considered the culprit. It was quite funny. Imagine my parents: they were sitting at the picnic table and enjoying their wine as their son was brought back by the other kids after two pints of shandy and flustered from his trip into the bushes.

Today, now my balance is even worse, people make comments such as "he looks like a drunk ..." I even often make that kind of joke myself. It makes people laugh and I laugh along - not only because laughter is infectious - but also because I simply really need to laugh about it all. It must look hilarious! It also breaks the tension. Of course sometimes it really isn't so amusing for me. But in that moment I ignore it and laugh my head off when I see the faces of people or imagine what they are thinking. Laughing at myself, knowing that something is wrong with me, has become my best medicine and has helped me to become more laid-back about things. Retaining my sense of humour and self-mockery is one of the most important things to me. Sometimes I even ask myself whether I am not being serious enough because so many situations end up in laughter. For example, my mother looks at me hesitantly but hopefully, when she asks me whether I am able to hear something when I begin to dance while music is playing or when the telephone rings and I snap my head round as if I heard it (she doesn't know that I sometimes see it from the display). Well, I'm in stitches just thinking about it, and I laugh at every opportunity. I'm sorry, mum!

If I can no longer laugh about such things, well - there really must be something wrong with me. Once this actually was the case, but that is another story ...

Back in France we didn't take things too seriously and even I began to think that it was because of the alcohol. In any case it helped to play the drunk guy. Nevertheless, I could feel that there was something wrong. At 16 I didn't pay attention to it; I was more interested in meeting girls. But where did my hearing problems fit in? Then again, this wasn't so important - mum was quick with a temporary diagnosis...sometimes you could get lumps of wax in your ears. For about a year we were satisfied with this theory until nothing improved, but when things got worse. We went to see an ENT doctor. It was somewhat surprising to be told that the inside of my ears were fine. The hearing test, however, did show a deterioration in my hearing. This meant that the problem wouldn't be going away. "Well, great! Why can't all these stupid problems just get lost?!", I thought to myself. So we were sent for a CT scan to get to the bottom of the problem. There, someone spoke to me in confidence when my mother wasn't present. It was all gobbledegook to me and the report was forwarded to my family doctor. We let things be for a while, and I got on with my life.

Months later, I was in the middle of my final secondary

school exams. My doctor never discussed the contents of that letter with me whenever I came by, in which it stated that further investigations should be performed in order to clarify whether I did indeed have the condition they thought it possible I was suffering from. Today we know that I lost valuable time then. Without knowing it, the tumours in my head had the time to grow.

At the time, not knowing what was causing my poor hearing, I was very glad to find that I had been assigned a seat at the front of the class next to the loudspeaker during my English listening exam. This really was a joke for my classmates because they knew I had grown up with English and some complained. Screw them, I didn't care … I wanted to pass the exams and reckoned that I would continue my studies at a grammar school the following year where I could do my A-levels. With my school exams in the bag we went over to England for the summer holidays in a camper van but my state was not getting any better. I even discovered that my father had searched my tent for empty bottles, only to find just dirty washing. I can still remember a few rough trips on a moped, complete with yet more landings into the bushes. We decided to have a CT test done after the holiday. And then it started.

We went to the neurology department to find out what the radiologists were able to find out during the CT scan and then had a more precise MRI scan done. When we found out that tumours were the reason for my problems my mother was alarmed. I wasn't as worried as much. Imagine a 16 year old who is about to take a step into the future. And don't forget the girls!

Today, MRI scans and hospital visits are just part of life and hospitals have taken over from the football pitch as my second home. At the age of 17 I was diagnosed with a condition with the strange name of 'Neurofibromatosis type 2'. "Neuro-what?", we had absolutely no idea what it was and blindly followed the advice of the doctors. Feeling as if it were all quite surreal, uncomfortable emotions surfaced as we approached the entrance to the neurosurgery department. The simple question "Hmm … what to do?" from an anonymous doctor tore us away from our terrible thoughts and did not calm us at all. Just the word 'tumour' was terrifying, alien and shocking. A thousand questions ran through our heads and my parents were particularly concerned as they had already done some research themselves. No one knew about this neuro-thing … "Just what is it that is wrong with him? Not even the doctors know what to do next?" Helplessness crept in. Fear.

Today we know that it is always the same with NF2: You always know better with hindsight. What would have been if we had not gone to the men in white coats who often overestimate their abilities and instead had gone directly to the specialists? Would my life today be entirely different? In the following years we learnt a lot more about the condition. It is a very rare condition in which tumours grow throughout the entire nervous system. It is typical to have a tumour growing on both auditory nerves, left and right, which usually eventually leads to complete deafness, a deterioration in balance, damage to facial nerves and other paralyses. So right there, in the very command centre of all the other organs, where all possible functions of the body begin. Tumours in the spinal column and elsewhere can be just as dangerous. All of them need to be monitored regularly to observe the growth changes. Consideration of the symptoms, the patient's condition and observation of the patient are naturally also important in making a decision on the right course of treatment. This is usually removal or decreasing the size of the tumours during an operation. As a genetic defect is the cause there is currently no cure available. Perhaps in the future there will be … but not at the moment. And it is going to be a rocky road ahead towards it. In Germany, only a handful of surgeons are competent enough and actually know enough about the condition. They are often confronted with great challenges because it is not unusual for the patient to suffer deterioration and to suffer a reduction in quality of life during the progression of the condition even after an operation which has been declared a success. The symptoms of each individual patient are completely different from those of the next and so comparisons are pointless. "Ah, I had a tumour in that area too," people would often say, but this was as relevant to my particular circumstances as a crystal ball prediction would be about in the future. The condition can develop to be mild, moderate or serious in each different patient. No one can predict it.

Without knowing all of this, and with doctors who were unable to tell us any more, we sat there mostly preoccupied with the concern that "life expectancy may be shorter". That didn't make much difference to me, as long as my stupid hearing would eventually go back to normal. My thoughts were elsewhere and I also wasn't very interested. I was only interested in the fact that in two weeks I would be having an operation that came with a 50:50 chance of saving my sense of hearing. "It'll be fine," I thought. Since then, I have become more realistic. After two weeks of waiting it was finally time.

I packed my things for the hospital. The nurses on the ward were really nice.

Upcoming operations have, meanwhile, now become the normality; it always reminds me of going on holiday with just tracksuits in my luggage because they are easy to put on. It is bizarre how people arrive with suitcases and bags. What is always missing, though, are the happy faces full of anticipation; it is rare to see anyone smiling. After a few boring tests it became increasingly serious but I remained calm. On 22nd September 2003 I was pushed out of the room on the ward and into the operating theatre. This date is fixed firmly in my soul and carries so much meaning for me. Above all: goodbye. But also: new beginnings.

It still moves me to tears to think about how things have changed since then, especially when I think about what is gone. Regardless of how I deal with it today, that day divided my life into a 'before' and an 'after'. How could I have known that at the time? I could cry every day. But I am also proud. Proud of where I have come from. Proud that I have decided to take control of my own fate, instead of struggling against it, to take it with me in my fight. At the time I didn't have the chance to say goodbye to my old life because I didn't realise that it was changing. It was probably better that way. I also didn't realise, as I was pushed out of my room, that I had already received the anaesthetic. When I woke up, my life had been turned on its head and once again I didn't yet know it.

Career start

Ten days later. I never ask them. I simply don't want my family to live through this period again, even in memory. It's beyond the power of my imagination to comprehend what it must feel like to live with the absence of a family member. My greatest fear is losing one of them. What was it like for my family when I was lying in intensive care? To know that I was lying unconscious and completely disconnected from the outside world, while my life was in the hands of a man who operated on my brain? I don't want to know. What a horrible experience it must have been for them.

Luckily I don't remember much of what seemed to have happened to me. Still, those nightmares I experienced are impregnated in my soul, and when they enter my consciousness I block each memory out before they begin to haunt me. The drugs that were administered during the eleven-hour operation and during the recovery period caused these hallucinations. I can't recall exactly what happened and when, the incidents are blurred. What I do remember, though, is being pushed through a sort of structure that was made out of millions of small orange coloured hexagons. The structure held my body firmly in place, moved automatically and tried to separate my mind from my body. As I forced my head through, the doctors appeared to be standing on the other side and shouted, "Don't do it! Don't do it!" Sure, I could ask myself what all this meant. I think it happened at some point during the actual operation. But I think I know already: perhaps they were trying to stop me from deciding to give up. As soon as

I was half awake there was no end to the nightmares and I couldn't distinguish my dreams from reality. I believed that I was witnessing a fight between one gang of colour and another gang and it was happening right next to me. It was about drugs and shots were fired. The bullets even entered my room and reached the black guy who was lying in the bed next to me. Tyres screeching, gunshots and shouting were audible.

The nightmares were such an awful experience; but the less I think of them, the more my memory of them disperses with time.

Once I imagined my sister was standing by my bed; she had come to say a final goodbye. But when I asked her about it later she was confused and denied it.

A nurse from intensive care put drops of water on my tongue. All I remember is that she was rather brusque and looked like an owl but those drops of water saved me and being given them was the only positive experience during that time. Later on I found out that my swallowing nerves had been slightly damaged; I was fed artificially because I couldn't take food or water orally.

The days passed by and slowly but surely I understood more of what was happening around me, what was happening to me and what had happened. I remember my mother grinning broadly after it initially appeared that my hearing hadn't been affected.

Back in my room on the ward I had occupational therapy and physio and all kinds of stuff at my bed. On TV I saw my then favourite football team, VfB Stuttgart, defeat Manchester United. I had such a good time watching the match but I would've preferred to play football again myself. Back then I wasn't aware that my career as a recreational footballer was over. I wanted to go outside; I wanted to get active. And every time the Burger King adverts appeared on TV, I'd melt: hunger had really started to set in. During a fortnight of compulsory fasting, I had lost almost 15 and half pounds.

Day by day I became more aware of my situation: I was in a fragile state of mind; I had lost hope and my life appeared to be falling apart. When I tried to stand up one day I asked the nurse why I always tilted to one side. "Because your balance nerves are damaged".

Oh well, I'll cope with that as well! I thought I was a complete wreck but things got even worse. During my stay in hospital, the rest of my hearing disappeared and I became completely deaf. A pen and paper were now to hand on the table next to my bed. I felt far away from my family and friends, even though they stood next to me. Later I discovered that people whose hearing is impaired often feel exactly the same. It's like being imprisoned but you're free. It's just like being behind a plate glass window.

Despite the circumstances, I was steadily getting better each day. On the ward I was given yoghurt to eat. My ability to swallow was actually improving. "Why only a little bit of yoghurt?", I wanted to know. "Because your swallowing nerves are damaged." And what about eating something like steak that I really loved? Well, I can eat a bit but it takes longer and my chewing muscles tire long before I'm full because steak has a difficult texture to break down. I therefore choose carefully what I eat to make sure I'm full and so that I don't lose weight. That also means that I might have to send the waitress away a number of times, but that's not my problem – and I don't want to get stressed about it. I also choke a lot because of my dama-ged trigeminal nerve, the cranial nerve that is responsible for the sensation of biting and chewing (somewhere a tumour is sitting on it). As it has been there for a while, the masticatory muscles have started to weaken. Particularly problematic is dry food, such as biscuits, and fluids. It was as if all these small setbacks were trying to bring me down.

As so much happened at once, I never got around to ques-tioning the purpose of the operation, as it seemed to only make things worse. Never did it occur to me that my condition would stay the same. At that time I didn't know that it could have been significantly worse. I also wasn't aware until later on that the surgeon had made the decision to remove only 30% of my left tumour. I'm glad because any more would've been too much. It had all become too much. I already felt comple-tely ruined as it was. I don't hold anything against the sur-geon, although he operated on me despite lacking in expertise. Only later when I was more informed about my condition did I realise that very few NF2 experts actually exist in Germany. Today I have mixed feelings about everything. First of all, I'm thankful that at such a young age he didn't burden me with an even greater challenge. Still, why did he choose to operate on me if he didn't have sufficient knowledge of NF2? I think he should have known better but those thoughts aside, he was a wonderful person and I'm sure he did his best. Anyway, my gratitude far outweighs my disappointment: who knows, may-be he saved my life? In any case, he could've damaged a lot more in those early days with NF2, but he didn't.

I began to write a list. The list comprised of things I wanted to do after being released from this horrible prison. At the top of the list was "eat sushi" and at the bottom was "learn to drive".

Departure

After being discharged from hospital, I went straight to a rehabilitation centre for young people in the far south of Germany. Of course, they were overwhelmed by my condition and my parents realised that it wasn't the right place for me to get back on my feet. But what I did take away with me was shown to me by my assigned 'guide' there: I was not alone with my fate. He introduced me to a Germany-wide online self-help group for NF2ers. In this way, I came into contact with Lorenz, who had already put up with the disorder for a number of years, and who has since then become a good friend. Meanwhile at home conversations and discussions followed by chatting online. Many times Lorenz brought me down to earth with his dry, realistic and yet humorous manner, while I, as is my nature, looked optimistically at the future. It was at this point that I decided to distance myself a bit by ignoring my illness and by focusing on living.

In fact at home things improved. It went from eating sushi with my closest circle of friends to receiving things to eat that had previously been denied. The Schwartz family, with whom I frantically communicated by paper at the restaurant, remain loyal to me to this day. Nico, a few years younger than me and one of my best friends, never left my side. And Ali, who I grew up with, is on the same wavelength as me. And there's John, yeah, who I thrash at English scrabble again and again. And I'll never forget Claudias Spaghetti from my childhood.

One day I discovered a stunning PC in my bedroom; something I would never ever have owned before. It was supposed to make communicating with the outside world easier for me. Miraculously, I regained some of my hearing on the left, operated side. I received audio therapy, practiced lip reading, and learnt how to cope with my situation and a hearing aid extracted even more from my residual hearing. What an incredible experience it was to finally find a hearing aid at the audiologist's that actually helped! Out of sheer unfamiliarity with a hearing aid device, I made the mistake of inadvertently leaving it on while having a shower. But it only happened once! Years later, after the hearing aid no longer worked, and consequently I no longer wore one, I still touched the back of my ear instinctively sometimes to see whether I had forgotten to remove it. However the more time that passed not wearing one, the more I got used to it; and today it's just a fleeting thought at best.

My hearing got better and better thanks to the hearing aid. One day my therapist, who supported me through this difficult time, held a piece of paper in front of her mouth so that I couldn't see her lips. Through hearing alone I understood the simple phrase that she had said! Increasingly often, communicating with my physiotherapist turned out well - even if I didn't look at her.

My PC actually became a communication device, made possible by the Internet. By using chat software and visiting chat rooms, I had found a means of communication that was no longer possible in the "outside" world. Eventually communicating in that way was 100% effective and it was without prejudice. Gerald, another NF2 sufferer, equipped me with basic PC skills that I pass onto others today. Deeper and deeper I sank into the isolation of the screen; I buried myself in virtual worlds where, in contrast to my real life, communication ran smoothly. The nights grew long. My parents understood but at the same time they didn't. I no longer noticed how often I left Manuel, the boy from next door, to kick a ball around alone in the garden.

My parents and I went on a sign language course. I learned fast and my parents did well too, considering being amongst a bunch of young student learners on the course. My father practised and practised by using, for instance, handmade index cards that he had made at work. Today, sign language has become a significant foundation of our relationship; at least, when I'm at home. It's an amazing achievement for my family. I have been (and am) extremely lucky.

An important moment was when I came into contact with the culturally Deaf who have never been able to hear. I thought I had found my identity again; I could finally join in with conversations again using sign language. That's what I thought, anyway. Little by little, I realised that many Deaf people are really quite different from us deafened individuals. For us, the loss of hearing often marks above all a dramatic turning point in life because your life is cut in two. An identity crisis is inevitable. For the Deaf, being deaf is often not such a big thing because they've grown up with it and they don't really know how it is to experience the world with the help of their ears... For some, that's completely normal, virtually as normal as body height, so they can't miss the hearing world. And they often grow up in the Deaf community: an amazing fraternity that's defined by sign language. From an early age, strategies would've been developed for them and their right place in society would've been found. Places and groups where they feel comfortable would have long since been discovered. A culture of its own develops from this and I don't really fit in. (I recognised this after a process that lasted a few years). Disagreement followed disagreement with the Deaf, despite them always welcoming me with open arms. I learned to appreciate them and I'm thankful that I've got to know their culture. Even today, I can't really get on that well with many of them who've decided to remain primarily in the Deaf community. But as is the case with most people, they are all very different. Today, I consider Alex, Annika and other Deaf individuals to be some of my best friends. Sometimes I ask myself, "Would it have been better to be Deaf, without having the memory of being able to hear, and therefore having experienced no loss?" No. I think it's a good thing that I grew up as a hearing individual. Since then I no longer ask myself that question.

I find that if I want to spend my time enjoying somebody's company we need to speak the same language. Sign language has proved to be a wonderful means of expression for me; it's also given me a door into the Deaf community. I could now sort of be a part of it. Since becoming deafened, sign language has become an integral part of my identity. I don't know how I'd manage without it now.

After quite a long time, which I needed and used to find myself again, I started to teach sign language to my close friends. They were happy to find a way back to connecting with me and thus my true self. At university I also founded a sign language society which quickly grew to be a central part of my studies. Today I make sure that my immediate environment is constructed so that sign language is a part of it. I feel naked and alone without it; that's why I'm eternally grateful for what this language has given and continues to give me.

However in public or with people I hardly know I'm shunned again and again; it's almost impossible to meet new people. I can understand only too well why quite a few of the Deaf decide to not even try to establish or nurture contacts with the hearing world and instead remain comfortably amongst themselves where everything works out. Actually, it's the same old frustrations with these "tactless hearing people". More often than not, it seems to me that a problem is created where one doesn't exist but that's an issue that I've resigned myself to long ago. A good example is the question, "What? You're allowed to drive a car although you can't hear anything? What happens if someone behind you beeps the horn?" Through gritted teeth I explain yet again that firstly 90% of car horns are sounded unnecessarily and secondly, the hard of hearing are actually better drivers because they are less distracted, they concentrate more and they are more alert. Understanding nods. "Right, next question?", I ask.

When amongst hearing people I see again and again how fast relationships develop under "normal" circumstances and how slowly they develop with me in comparison. It's most painful when I see how different the same situations are played out. For example, after two minutes we're still on names, while somewhere else someone screams, "Oh yeah! I know James too …!"

It's worse being in a group but I've learnt to put the breaks on; to distance myself instead of just sitting there and watching the whole thing. I realised later that it also has to do with me. I weigh up whether my efforts would be worth it or not. I decide whether the person is a potential friend or merely a fleeting contact. If I see potential in someone I would get active and come up with various strategies; especially if the potential someone was female and I liked her...

Many people are so overwhelmed by unusual communicative situations that they'd rather turn the other way or say nothing at all. This, of course, is clearly the easiest solution for them. Despite every missed opportunity being like a slap in the face for me I've gotten used to the silence. It's interesting to see how many people are afraid of failure. So it's up to me to build the largest part of the communication bridge. These situations (or non-situations) can also be positive: finally no more meaningless blahblahblah and gossip, instead it's straight to the essentials and often much more interesting topics. A simple direct approach, just like sign language naturally is, can be really efficient. Many people confront their helplessness by running away and they often don't even realise that they've hurt me by doing so. However, I don't think I'd have reacted any differently in their position. A comment such as, "no matter", or, "it's not important", is a stab in the heart. And for me, the person who decides to reply like that, shines a little less brightly in my eyes. It's as if I'm not worth the effort. I always try not to take it personally. And when I think it over, I'm certain that it's not me they're avoiding but the unfamiliar communicative situation that they're having with me. I also tell myself again and again, "That's their loss, not mine." That's because I like myself and the people who are important to me like me too. However, it's also my loss. Even a bit of small talk and seemingly trivial interpersonal contact opens doors. But these doors often remain closed for me; it makes me feel detached from personalities, information, interpersonal relations and from having access to people in general. Simply from the colours, the variety, all aspects of life. Instead it seems that contact with strangers always goes the same way, as so much of the conversation is concealed. An example: In hospital I asked at reception whether football was being shown somewhere on TV that evening. I got talked at constantly for two minutes without being given an opportunity to reply. Then I said that I was deaf and I asked the receptionist if he could please write it down. That was obviously too stupid a thing for him to do as he shook his head and simply replied, "no", he didn't know. So, our conversation was reduced to the essentials and further information, interpersonal communication and the notion of possibility was lost. What had he actually said? Had he talked about the match because it interested him? Or had he said that a large firework would be set off in the garden tonight? Anyway, I ask strangers questions less and less often.

There are fortunately more and more people everywhere who don't follow this pattern of behaviour, which paradoxically, is particularly outside my comfort zone because that's where the magic happens. Each time I go up to someone I have to be brave, but I quickly feel rewarded for having taken the step.

Due to the countless communicative situations that pass me by, my thoughts always revolve around my experiences and I: I'm quickly turning into a damned egocentric! Perhaps that's also a reason for writing this book. It makes me feel like a fish trapped in the never changing fish tank. How often would I love to know which languages were being spoken around me. But, instead of focusing on what I can't do I often try to look for things that I can do. For example, I guess nationalities by someone's accent, which I can recognise by lip reading. (For some reason, I find people with accents easier to lip-read.)

Nevertheless, many situations reveal what I can no longer do. But getting angry because of all of these things would be a waste of my energy. Sadness, disappointment and frustration often remain and very often I have to be careful that these emotions don't pull me down. In order to preserve my precious open mind it helps to find other doors and to open them.

So, by reprogramming what I expected from life and what I could expect of myself in a new way, I felt more secure and it felt like I was on the right path. Even if many changes in my attitude only happened later on, I began to sense it. A psychologist describes the process using the metaphor of a vase: The vase falls onto the floor and is shattered. Now I have a choice. Do I throw the vase away and lose it forever? It will never look the same as before and even if it's stuck back together it will always be very fragile. Or, do I take the pieces and build something new, like a mosaic?

The time to accept that my life will never be the same as before and to recognise that I can, nonetheless, build something new and beautiful lay ahead of me, overlaid with grief and a state of denial. Yet, step by step I began to build my own mosaic, to cut my own path and to pick the flowers that defied adverse conditions by deciding to grow in patches between the stones. I also got my driver's license in this year; so soon I'd be able to make my own way driving.

Munich

The plan to take my A-levels was quickly buried. It was simply impossible to have an inclusive education at a normal school. So we looked for alternatives and found a boarding school for the hearing impaired in Munich. I checked out the Grammar school there and the College of Further Education next to it. A week at the CFE was enough for me to say, "Bring it on!"

When arriving at the boarding house, I came into contact with a future 'tutor' Ulla, who told me later of her first and positive impression of me. This changed, however, when she saw me staggering about the next morning. Years later she said that she had pigeonholed me in the bottom drawer with the "boozers" and had thought, "Oh my God, what's wrong with him? Is he already drunk first thing in the morning?" She had pondered over this for a long time until a discussion over my symptoms provided clarification.

Of course, I experience non-stop prejudice. I look into horror-stricken faces with amusement when someone helps me into the driver's seat of a car. Even better if there are two people propping me up in the dark! But no one ever stopped me from climbing into the driver's seat. Why should I care what other people think of me? The people who are important to me know the score. Other people's reactions often reveal more about themselves than about me. Besides, prejudices are actually quite normal; they belong in my thoughts, too. Far too often unfortunately. I'd even dare to assert that it's precisely these prejudicial thoughts of others that help me 'pick' the 'good' people, those who are open with me.

Barely one year after what I refer to as my, "lightening bolt", I moved into a room in Munich. It was a good moment to live away from home, semi-independently, anyway. I quickly made friends. Meeting my educator Anne Bouwmeester from Holland (the name "Anne" can also be masculine in Holland) was like winning the jackpot. He always had an open ear for my complaints about the Deaf, the hearing and about my place in the world but philosophical subjects, such as football, also moved us both. Being a FC –Bayern Munich hater, confrontations and discussions with other residents were part of everyday life. Of course, football matches were watched on TV, cushions were thrown and Ulla even had to put us all in our place once.

And so, I began to heave myself back on track, having distanced myself from NF2; my ignorant attitude meant that I didn't really understand the extent of the condition nor had I really considered the potential outcome. Of course there were restrictions but nothing too serious. Thanks to my ruined balance, I'd got used to being the last team member selected for the indoor football match every week; in the past I'd been selected fairly early on. I was increasingly surprised at how seriously the others took the game, "they should just be happy they can move around normally!", I thought.

I didn't have many concerns in terms of communicating within this setting. The number of Deaf people I made contact with notably increased because I was in a class for the Deaf at the CFE. It was a fantastic time and my NF left me in peace. The fact that a growing tumour made me lose my voice at some point within a week and meant that I could only speak hoarsely was annoying but it didn't bother me too much. After having a consultation with my NF2 doctor (I was by that time in expert hands) in Wurzburg I found out that research was being conducted on an implant in order to emulate the function of a larynx. For me that meant patience; it'll be fine. Just a bit longer to wait…

At the end of the year we drove to Holland with Anne's group of students (around 7). Everyone had a bike and Anne was with me on a tandem. Being in the saddle once again felt so good that I blocked out not being able to ride the bike myself. We cycled around the North Sea island Schiermonnikoog on our fiets along the fietspad on Bloedstraat. After a refreshment in the Lindeboom guesthouse and on the way back on our bicycles we got caught in an unforgiving downpour. While the others sought refuge in a nearby barn, I got my Frisbee out and with my powers of persuasion, I succeeded in inciting at least one of the Bouwmeester group to play Frisbee in the rain. Sometimes there's nothing left to do than to make the most out of a situation.

I have always been a know-it-all. Even my roommates at boarding school started to feel the force of it sometimes. At these times one bedroom door or another slammed shut yet again. It was a miracle no one lost a finger. When playing FIFA, however, my gamepad had to bite the dust. (Why doesn't the stupid defender go there!?) After I had fired it against the wall it didn't work anymore. Oops! Winning streaks alternated with losing streaks. Well, OK, overall my Deaf friends Harry and Thomas were at the same skill level as me. We agreed on a draw. As a newcomer to the Deaf community, I didn't find my feet straight away and I made a mistake that so many people make by saying, "But they're dumb". Only later did I learn that they're not dumb but simply different. Of course I didn't make any friends with such a statement. How many people have thought similar of me: that I'm dumb just because I don't understand or I don't get something? In spite of that, I tried to integrate myself as a deafened person. As communicating with the Deaf worked out best for me, I kept finding myself talking in sign language more and more. I was lucky enough to learn it going along. But still, it wasn't my world and I sometimes felt like a misfit. Now and again it hurt to see how the Deaf or hard of hearing formed groups; I could dip into groups but more than that wasn't possible. Compared to the others, my door was rarely knocked on. Maybe I just didn't hear it. Ha ha?

On the other hand, I had the opportunity to take someething away for me from everywhere. It's still like that today. I move between the edges of two worlds. Whether I find it a positive or negative experience depends on my mindset, and of course, it often hurts too. Nonetheless, I generally try to see things in a positive light. I've already been very lucky to have grown up with two languages. Thanks to my British mother, who only spoke English to me, I have a four-fold identity. I'm a real Gemini but I've been doubled, she states again and again with a chuckle on her lips. And then I smile too, as that's exactly what I like, isn't it? To be a little bit special and not just Mr Joe Bloggs. I think it's alright that way! I've always been a bit of a lone wolf.

I still remember when a couple of the hard of hearing students from the boarding school sat together one evening and smoked a hookah. I naturally wanted to smoke with them and I sat down. It tasted slightly unusual so I asked what was in it. One of the hearing impaired answered (he didn't know any sign language). I only understood something with the sound "O". He only knew half of the finger alphabet and I don't know whether it was his mistake or mine; but anyway, I got onto my knees immediately and wanted to stop breathing. COKE! Oh God, I didn't want that! I looked around, huffing and puffing in panic. "Did you say coke?" Yet again he didn't understand me correctly and said calmly, "yep!" That went on a bit longer until I worked out that he had said "coco(nut)". Phew!

I felt fairly under-challenged by the lower standard in the Deaf class, so I moved to a class with only a few hearing students of which only two other students were slightly hard-of-hearing. With the help of technical equipment and the support of the teaching staff, together with cooperative fellow students, we could tickle just enough of my then residual hearing so that I could more or less follow what was going on; and from there on it led to the final exams and to OA Levels.

My goal of getting A-levels had been reached, sort of. Admittedly, the FCE wasn't altogether my ideal place to study, but by then I had got used to that. I look back fondly at my school days.

Mode of expression

While the poems that I wrote during my childhood centred on my friends, Spaghetti or Santa Clause, it turned out that in later years I often wrote about social criticism. I described situations and wrote dedications for others...the medium of poetry has become my mode of expression ever since I was little.

In some poems, English is the original language, in others German. When these were translated, unfortunately I had to drop the rhyme, accepting the limits of translation. However, for those readers who speak both languages I will add the German original underneath. For those who don't know German and still want to give reading them a try: yes, it's a strange language ;-)

In the Munich years I busied myself with other things again. When I could, I pursued things that I had previously been interested in. It was still painful that I couldn't do sport properly, yet there was now a load of people in the boarding house who played my beloved ultimate Frisbee, having been inspired by me and instigated by one of the tutors. Or Tichu – not sport either – but the best card game ever!

Hope

Is there a future without killing?
What would this world be like?
No matter, it's needed desperately!
Not sometime, but right now!

And in what kind of world do we live in?
Why do people have to suffer?
In a world full of hate and greed.
Can't war be avoided?

Where is the role model that shows us,
that there's also love, in another sense?
But this model is silent
And the world which loves, it parts

Do soldiers die for their country?
Why suffering, why war?
The real reason is obvious:
It's about power and victory.

But power can be shown in a different way!
By acting clever and cooperation.
But this power will remain silent.
Man today just seeks confrontation.

Words are often the same false path
Well, better than war, you can learn from them
But words are often just as narrow
Leading to the same outcome

The answer can be sought forever
But can't be found
You can also blame those guilty
The weak light is called hope.

(NB: This poem was inspired by the Iraq war)

German Original:

Hoffnung

Gibt es Zukunft ohne Töten?
Wie wäre dieser Welt' Gestalt?
Egal, sie wäre so von Nöten!
Und zwar nicht später, sondern bald!

Und In welcher Welt leben wir?
Warum müssen Menschen leiden?
In einer Welt voll Hass und Gier.
Kann man Krieg nicht meiden?

Wo ist das Vorbild, das uns zeigt,
dass es auch Liebe gibt, in anderem Sinn.
Doch dieses Vorbild schweigt
Und die Welt die sich liebt, scheidet dahin.

Sterben Soldaten für ihr Land?
Warum Töten, warum Krieg?
der wahre Grund liegt auf der Hand:
Es geht um Macht und den großen Sieg.

Doch Macht kann man auch anders zeigen!
Durch kluges Handeln und Kooperation.
Doch diese Macht wird ewig schweigen.
Der Mensch von heute sucht nur Konfrontation.

Worte sind oft auch der falsche Weg.
Zwar besser als Krieg, man lernt was daraus.
Doch Worte sind oft auch ein schmaler Steg
und dieser führt auf dasselbe hinaus.

Die Antwort kann man ewig suchen,
doch fündig wird man nicht.
Man kann auch die Schuldigen verfluchen.
Hoffnung heißt das schwache Licht.

Some poems were and still are a form of processing in which emotions can be given expression. Others come from puns are spontaneous expressions of my creativity. It seems to me that it's a sign of me feeling well, whenever I write such silly poems for fun, just like I used to in my childhood.

Childhood. Once again, a key word that's full of a lot of feelings. I think that's the same for many people. Anyway, I'm really lucky to have enjoyed an exceptional childhood and no one can take that away from me. Despite being over, it has become my greatest treasure. I've taken Ghandi's wise words as a motto for life, "Don't cry because it's over, smile because it happened."

Most of the poems written in later years - found now and again here between the main text of this book - often come from the depths of my soul and that's how I convey my feelings.

Kaboom the Doom

When fate decides to play its card
Comes into life without a warning
And you give up or you die hard
Or you spend all day with mourning

Hey, then something isn't right!
You have to be strong and proud
You should not stop the fight
Don't be weak and quiet, no, be loud!

Show your middle finger
To every sign of grief
It's not worth to let it linger
Create your own belief

Accept the challenge, yes, take it
Believe in yourself, be positive
Tolerate your destiny and face it!
And your attitude will be causative

Over the years, I accepted my destiny more and more, and I took part in a yearly summer gathering for people who share the same condition as me. Even if I haven't been as seriously affected as many other people, and despite the initial shock of what the illness can do to people, it was simply great. Finally a place where I could be myself. So "normal", like nowhere else. I ought to compose a poem about it later.

The stone

So in the meantime I just tried to accept how things are, be it a mere shower. "Oh, come on, It's only water!" has become my standard reply when someone complains that it's raining. Grey expressions always turn into a smile. That was worth it, wasn't it? In the past I joined in with complaints about the winter, until my brother once said, "The winter is only bad in your head". That really made me think, and since then I've tried to like the essence of each season equally. Not very easy! I once read about someone who came to Europe from a country where the climate was always the same, and when asked what he liked best about Germany he answered, "the seasons". Suddenly I understood what a gift it is to be able to experience this natural spectacle afresh each year.

I still remember - it was at some point after the start of my NF2 career - when our friend Brigitte told me the story of the palm tree and the stone. The beautiful story is about a young palm tree whose development is disrupted and nearly destroyed when a stone is thrown into the heart of its crown by a passer-by. The fatally wounded plant is seized by uncontrollable pain and a hopeless lack of strength. Shaking off the stone doesn't work; it wants to be and must be accepted by the palm tree. Eventually "a small wave of strength" stirs in the young palm tree, and it begins to grow in spite of the pain and in spite of fate. From then on, the palm sapling centres all its strength on surviving with the weight of the stone; it accepts the stone as being a part of itself and it continues to grow. Despite being different from the other palm trees, it becomes stronger and more powerful over time until, safe and secure under its powerful leaves, life pulsates around it.

It was still too soon after the diagnosis for me to make any use of the story; I didn't even try to shake off the stone. I don't even know if I got anything from the story, as it didn't really interest me. I pretended that a stone wasn't even there. When the story fell into my hands again years later - I had by this time accepted my fate - I immediately understood what Brigitte had wanted to tell me. That's how I began to identify myself with the story, and each time I read it, my eyes fill with tears.

I would soon have my OA-levels in the bag as well. I was determined to start studying in England afterwards. The final decision came during the summer when we were on our way back from Cornwall in the camper van. We drove past Southampton where my cousin Samantha studied at that time, I just thought to myself: "A city next to the sea? Fishing every day! Great!" At the campsite I met a bilingual English and Spanish speaker. As so many people speak Spanish, I thought it would be a good way to be equipped to travel the world and to talk to people. Consequently, it became clear to me what I would study.

But my NF2 was still there. After my OA-levels it would've been a good time to operate on the enormous tumours in my head: the tumours that still compressed my brainstem. A lot was at risk. It was serious business. But I didn't get that, or I didn't want to. I felt reasonably good, didn't I? My residual hearing on my left side was stable. So I decided to wait. A mistake? Probably. In hindsight... oh yeah, I already said. So, the tumours had more time to grow, the pressure on my brainstem increased and irreversible damage was caused. I know that now. In magazine interviews I often read the following question, "If you could turn back the clock and could do something differently, what would it be?" Of course I could now answer, "I would've had the operation immediately". But I don't say that because I'm trying to live my life without regrets. Back then there was a reason for my decision, even if it's hard for me to comprehend it now. I stand by my reasoning and my (wrong) decision. Every decision made by each person feels like the right one in that very moment, doesn't it? That's just how it was then. I'm interested in what's happening now and what I can do with it.

As the operation was off the table for now I went to Southampton to learn Spanish. The support that I was given there meant that it was definitely within the framework of my possibilities. I thought to myself, "Why should being deafened hinder you?" I simply continued with my plans, even if they were a bit different from how I'd imagined them to be. Luckily student support for the disabled is really good in England, especially my note-taking support, which was my lifeline. Those notetakers sat next to me and wrote speedily on their note pads or tapped on their laptops, so that even if I missed a lot, I was still almost on equal footing with the rest of the class. I dived into another world: being a student was great. Three months things ran smoothly, but then I was bought back down to earth with the reality of the situation: my hearing was stable but my balance was slowly getting worse. I went home for Christmas and also for a renewed talk with my surgeon. Fear for the future knocked at my door again; the major operation had clawed its way back to the table again. Can't I simply sweep it away? Again and again I found myself weighing up the pros and cons; I had now realised that a lot was at stake. After a lot of toing and froing, I finally decided to have the operation. We set our sights on having it in January, with the prospect of improving my balance and of having an implant, which ought to allow me to hear at least sounds, as my residual hearing would bow out during the surgery. This time I at least had a little time to prepare myself for my renewed "farewell", and I realised that having more time is no better than less. I began to slide into a depression. Nothing interested me anymore and everything reminded me of the forthcoming operation. I noticed how many sounds there were in the world and was reminded by each one that it may be the last time I would hear them naturally. According to the surgeon my facial nerves would probably be destroyed during the operation. That would mean that I would no longer be able to smile. Looking back to that period, I didn't really feel like smiling anyway; and I started to long for the operation, to have it behind me. Back then I summarised my thoughts in the following way:

"At the moment my facial nerves still allow me to smile, but my heart doesn't, as this time it seems like the world is sinking and I'm live on show as it happens. And yet, my untiring fighting spirit of NF2 matters says, "you can't give up", and I don't have the heart to do it anyway. NF2 might defeat me, but I won't do anything myself. And even if I have to battle with the fear of dying: now that I've slowly grasped the seriousness of the situation and now that the news of other NF2ers dying hits me like a ton of bricks. But nevertheless every day I play enforced optimism and I tell people that I'll see them in England again soon. My story is far too long to come out with the truth; namely that I don't really believe anymore that I'll be able

to continue my studies in England. Anyway, it takes an enormous effort to tell the same rubbish again and again and then to see how people distance themselves from me so that they can continue with their wonderful lives. But it's OK; I'd be the same. At the moment my thoughts are on the operation and I don't think any further than that, as it seems so unbelievable that I'll be able to undertake much afterwards. I mentally prepare myself for my departure from the world as I know it, or have known it, and all I'll be able to do is live an online presence. At least I've got that. What did NF2 sufferers do before the internet? Indeed, it could always be worse, and that's the last straw I can hold on to. At least I can live out my mind a little on the Internet. A mind imprisoned in a sickly body. Anyhow, I think I've done everything right. I held myself back from the NF2 group and have up until now lived as normally as possible. I confront the various things that other NF2 sufferers complain about with the motto: 'What I don't know won't hurt me'.

The fact is, is that I make other people who have small, or in my opinion ridiculous, aches and pains happy. Sure, I'm glad about that, but it also makes me realise what's in it for me and that is actually NOTHING (NB: I wouldn't say that today anymore!). I'm still sitting in my trap. Uplifting words are all very nice but they fall far short of reality. "It'll be OK". But OK, what else could someone say? It's best to say nothing. Just let me suffer alone and at some point the period of suffering will be over".

The decline in my mood was terrible. During this period I was lucky to have the support of my family: my sister and her baby, and my parents who suffered with me. And even though in the end I had to be alone during the operation, they agreed that, "Together we are strong!" In one of my last blog entries before the operation my true nature flared up once more after having a conversation with my brother. In my most profound moments he is always there for me and steers me in the right direction:

"Even if my state of health changes, I'll still be the same person. I think I'm a good person and NF2 can never take that away from me".

And that was what carried me on my long and impending journey. My belief in myself had been wrapped up just in the nick of time. I also endured the video documentation of my still fully functioning face, while at the same time I just wanted to curl up and die. Finally the time had come and I was ready. And yet everything turned out differently, and afterwards the actual decent began.

Hell

Before the operation I only actually had two problems: I was very hard of hearing and had increasingly severe problems with balancing when walking. There were other small issues which didn't overly affect me, such as the fact that my voice was now weaker or that I now ate slower due to slight problems with swallowing. Among deafened people it wasn't an issue, it was completely normal that food got cold. Who can watch what they are doing with their knife and fork while at the same time watching others at the table in order to be able to keep up with the conversation? And then also sign themselves? Especially when the others are insisting that it had been an obvious penalty for FC Bayern Munich yesterday. Impossible! At the height of the discussion drinking glasses would go flying from being knocked over and I later learned to move my glass about a metre away from my signing radius. Vases of flowers and candles are also often in the way during conversations. Aesthetics and romance no longer stand any chance against practicalities at the dinner table. Even real, hand-picked flowers; they will be moved aside without mercy. The ideal environment needs to be created. Too dark in the pub? Then we'll just have to go to a different one.

My expectations of the operation were thus: I knew that the auditory nerve would likely be cut; that hearing naturally would no longer be possible. A remedy to this is what is known as an ABI - an Auditory Brainstem Implant - which is placed onto the brainstem in order to at least allow the wearer to hear sounds. Better than nothing is what I thought and I still think.

Just before the operation I learned that, "The ABI is the last thing on the list," whatever that meant. Ah well, whatever, I wasn't going to worry about it anyway. Almost two months after the surgery, after I had regained consciousness, I asked my parents from my bed: "Have I got an ABI in?" They just shook their heads. I was sad and cross, but they just said to me that it would be put in at a later date. I put on my old hearing aid, but even after I'd changed the batteries in a hopeful last-ditch attempt … Nope, it was gone.

But that was just a minor concern in comparison to the other post-surgery problems. After all, even if my face was quite crooked thanks to an "offended nerve", the surgeon had apparently been able to preserve the majority of my facial function. That was great but came to be a small consolation. "What use is a good face to me when everything else is fucked up?" I'd said at the time, not without anger. Today I am very grateful for an almost straight face. At the time, it was much worse not to be able to walk at all any more, for example. It was a big adjustment as I'd previously thought that my balance would improve. Instead, I found myself in a wheelchair; it felt like I'd lost some of my dignity. To begin with I couldn't even turn over in bed. Months later, after daily therapy, when I was finally allowed out, my family and friends at rehab took me to an aquarium in the outside world which had seemed so far away. Unreachable. I had wandered into the hospital before the operation with what appears to me now as an optimistic naïvety. "This isn't going to be much different from my first operation in 2003," I'd thought to myself. I have since become much more cautious and realistic. Nevertheless, that optimism has stayed with me. It is a balancing act, never wanting or expecting too much, but at the same time I know that if I didn't want any more, then nothing would change. Now, before each procedure, my motto is: 'Expect the worst. Hope for the best!' This is not easy when nothing is very predictable. It's quite ironic to be speaking of a balancing act when you have lost your ability to balance isn't it? Oh well, that's just how it is.

Back to the surgery: My first surgery, which at the time had seemed big with a recovery time of around a year, I would learn was peanuts in comparison with the second. It started on the intensive care ward; in 2003 I had woken up a few days after the surgery and 'only' my hearing had changed. Other things, such as difficulties swallowing, 'quickly' recovered - after a month I left the hospital to continue my convalescence at home. This time, as I was to find out, I spent six weeks in intensive care after having a tracheotomy to assist me with breathing, being unable to hear, asleep (as well as a week in an induced coma) and still having these horrible nightmares – only they were even worse and I was having many more of them.

I only found out what had really happened after that in bits and pieces in between times of unconsciousness. I was absolutely convinced that I was dead, I saw my own funeral, saw myself being carried through Wurzburg in Bavaria to the funeral in a horse-drawn carriage, although somehow I was body-less as I couldn't feel it. Only a head in a glass box. In fact, dreams and reality were once again becoming mixed and the dreams were unimaginably terrible. I slowly began to realise that someone in a green jumper was there and later found out that it had been my sister. I was visited every day, which I could hardly believe later on. I have no memories of any of the visits. Where was I?

My family began to write down what I said. Today, I have

pushed most of my memories from during that time out of my consciousness, and I know there is more I did not memorise in the first place. I am amazed at how seemingly trivial some of the remarks were when it seemed to me as if my conscious mind was somewhere completely different. I remember the phrase: "I've been to hell and back!" Aside from being able to feel my head, I was still, weeks later, convinced that the rest of my body was 'dead'. My brother wrote the following down, which I apparently had said: "I need to die. You don't all see it, but I do. I want to die, but I can't. I need a knife so that I can stab myself in the heart." Later that same day, after my brother had hoisted my legs up and showed me that they were still there, I asked how VfB Stuttgart had played. "Only Bayern today", he said and I could immediately feel my middle finger stirring … When I asked the question of whether one of my nurses were a FC Bayern Munich fan and it turned out he preferred cycling sports, I replied: "Tour de Doping!" I was still able to make jokes, so maybe I was still there after all. "Now I've got a new chance", and, "I am a fighter", I had apparently also uttered. Well, then! A U-turn in the right direction and all within the space of a day. Once again my brother Pascal had saved me.

All this is over and done with. Over. I still don't know where I was or what I was supposed to do there. But it doesn't matter anyway, I am here now. That is all that counts. What I have taken from it all is very valuable today: Coming from such a low point, I know now that life is to be treasured and I am forever grateful that I am allowed to live, and it is precisely this experience that is the source of my strength and that of my companions. Through this experience, since I have fought, and gained back a lot, I now know today: It could be worse.

The hotel

Once I was transferred to the semi-intensive care unit, I started to become more alert and to understand more of what was going on around me, although not much. At least I was able to recognise my family. I had been brought to the neurological rehabilitation centre in Bad Neustadt. My old friend John suggested it was just 'like a hotel'. Our opinions of the place couldn't have been more different. He meant well and the rehab centre was indeed quite respectable.

But my time passed agonisingly slowly there amongst the pensioners, who were often recovering from a stroke. I can still remember when I left my room in a wheelchair for the first time and went past a table with most of people around it doing nothing but sitting there in silence. The nurse introduced me to the others and told them that I had lost my hearing and that they should write a message down if they wanted to communicate with me. I placed a pen and piece of paper on the table and the person sitting next to me grabbed them and started to write something down. After about two minutes he was still writing and I began to wonder why it was taking him so long. I glanced at the paper and saw nothing but scribbling. When the nurse passed by, she pointed to him and gestured something equivalent to 'he's gone bananas'. This is how it was with most of the other patients. It was a shame. He could keep the pen. In the future, I didn't take anything with me to write with anymore.

At least I didn't have to look at the same picture on the wall all the time. Once back in my room I longed for a nurse to come in to do something. Communication was basically impossible because she didn't have time to write anything down and I couldn't hear anything. But I didn't care, just anything!

It was still more interesting than lying there and doing absolutely nothing. Communicating on the intensive care ward consisted of giving a thumbs up or down, or by pointing to the few sentences about basic necessities which were written down on the paper that my dad had laminated: 'I have to use the loo', 'please turn me around', etc. Here at least, sometimes things were written down. One of the nurses even learned a little sign language from the finger alphabet poster my father put up over the bed. So even here, there were exceptions and I will never forget my nurse Vera for making an effort. Hardly anyone else attempted to use sign language. Instead, I spent my time watching biathlon, which in my opinion, has to be one of the most boring sports ever. My dad had put a television in my room to help me pass the time, but as it turns out biathlon is one of the few things that you can watch without subtitles. The alternative: ski-jumping.

Fortunately I was given a 'therapy schedule' with all the therapies for the week. My mom organised a visit from someone at least once a day and eventually I was allowed to leave my ward and go downstairs. They pushed me through the main entrance. The next time I made it to the adjacent building. There was something new to discover with each fresh 'step' forward. One building had an aquarium and it soon became my favourite spot. I went there nearly every day. One day, during her visit, Brigitte showed me the different flowers that began to sprout everywhere. On another day I went on a route that was way longer than my usual one. It was to the Italian restaurant down the road where my three visitors had something to eat. Towards the end of my stay I went out into the world with my father to the nearby town Neustadt an der Saale and enjoyed a little bit of ice cream, just like everyone else. Boy that was quite an experience–just being there.

I couldn't speak during my entire stay in the rehab centre. The tube in my throat didn't allow air to get into the upper respiratory tract which meant voice formation wasn't possible. The tube prevented saliva and food from getting into my lungs and yet, I still managed to get pneumonia about eight times, primarily while I was in the intensive care unit. These bouts of pneumonia repeatedly set me back in terms of my recovery. I usually developed pneumonia after something went down the wrong pipe and into my lungs, which brings me to my next point: food. Humans need it to survive and I was fed by a feeding tube inserted in my stomach because I couldn't swallow and I lacked the strength to eat. Attempts to eat food naturally with an occupational therapist failed time and time again, but at least it was a long-term goal. When my therapist said, "Next week, let's try a spoon of jelly", I'll admit that I looked forward to it a bit. My sense of smell was also gone. Nothing! One day when the tube was unblocked for a while, I could smell the typical chlorine smell from the swimming pool area. I savoured it as if it was the sweetest perfume.

As time went by the biggest loss in my quality of life was by far the inability to eat; it became clear to me what a luxury eating is and how much pleasure is derived from this simple act. Looking back I realise that not being able to do it anymore really was the worst. Instead I was fed high calorie nutrients through a feeding tube. I was never hungry. I watched how my visitors bit into their sandwiches and I think they asked me whether it would be OK if they ate something. And it was. I mean, if they were hungry...

In the past, my motto was 'What I don't know, doesn't hurt me', but it turned out to backfire. Let me give everyone new to NF2 a serious warning not to make the same mistake that I made and to get informed before it is too late. If I hadn't ignored NF2, and instead had understood the risks involved, I would have known that brainstem surgery can be extremely complex and the risks both numerous and severe. I should have given more careful thought to having the surgery in the first place. But self-reproach doesn't help here, I think it is something that many people with NF2 experience in their learning process. Had I been better informed, would it have changed my decision? What would my expectations have been? What if I had known what was ahead of me? Could anyone have even told me that before? Would it have helped? And what about my life without the surgery? Would that have made things better or worse? Would I even still be alive today?

Generally speaking, the 'could haves', 'should haves' and 'would haves' in this world have become my enemy. It seems like there is no escape from the hypothetical jungle, which is why I don't even try to wander around it and risk getting lost, except before an important surgery or decision that could lead to quite radical changes. That's the only way I can handle it. Besides, speculating doesn't lead to anything useful anyway.

The deep

It is no secret that for many who have NF2 there are times when you wish the earth would just swallow you up. "Would I not be free from my prison if everything were over?" That thought kept coming back to me. I think suicidal thoughts are familiar to a lot of us. I can't do anything about it, the thought is simply there. It can't do me any harm, though. In the end the decision is mine and now I ban those thoughts as soon as they appear. Periods of depression are also common and they have an impact; many people become trapped in these periods and remain depressed - this is no surprise as NF2 can be so horrible. Nevertheless, I don't know a single NF2-er that was so depressed that they ended their life. On the contrary, the worse they are affected, the stronger they seem to fight back. "Never give up, always keep fighting", is a motto they have internalised and each person fights in their own way. We are all in the same boat and at some point we will be able to see the shore. Others neither look ahead nor look back and feel completely contented. That's not me yet. Until someone shouts, "Land in sight!", many people seemingly tolerate the storm just by believing: "Life isn't about waiting for the storm to pass, it's about learning to dance in the rain." So we dance together which is great and it makes many things so much easier. What would I be today without this self-help group that Klaus and Helene Weber created? I can't imagine and I am forever grateful.

When I woke up from the second operation it was my body that had changed most of all; everything seemed broken. But there was also something inside me that wasn't right and would not get better even during the months of rehab - quite the opposite. When I was finally diagnosed, months later, with reactive depression I was at first relieved to be able to define the feeling. I didn't get better and I sank to my lowest point. It took so much energy to write down how I felt. If someone had said to me at the time: "This will end up in a book one day," I would have thought they'd lost their mind and probably tried to strangle them a little bit …

"I have no desire to do anything, no love of life. I don't want to do anything except sleep, every day I get up (unfortunately) and often check the time just to see when the day will finally be over. I just want everything to be over with quickly. I am unfriendly to others for no reason and don't enjoy anything. Other people annoy me, even neighbours and friends. I hate physiotherapy and don't think it's making any difference. In general, I don't think anything is doing any good at all. I can't be happy about anything. I can't learn anything new and think I am forgetting a few things. I only think about the negative things that other people have said to me. For example, my surgeon said to me word-for-word: "We need to do the right-hand side soon, too". This sort of thing is constantly whirring around my head and I can remember the negative things very clearly. I have no memory, I forget everything, I can't reminisce. I can't lie and only think about myself. I do answer emails etc., but only briefly and only about the important things. The depression is the worst of it all, I don't care that I can't eat (not that I wouldn't love to be able to eat). But the depression is worse than being completely deaf".

The neurological rehab, which was at a clinic about an hour away from home, was by and large a horrible experience. Not due to boredom. Actually, it should have been due to that. My lowest point was my depression. It gnawed away at me after all the setbacks and dragged me down even further so that eventually I could barely see the light anymore; I almost switched it off myself. But only almost. I made a miserable attempt to hold my razor under the water, but couldn't bring myself to do it and called the nurse. For my parents that was the sign that they needed to get me out of there and take me home.

Julia, who has since passed away, always wrote me things to cheer me up. She was just about the only one who could really say anything to me, after all she also had NF2 herself and was also struck down by the illness when she was young: "You are only given as much as you can handle," she once wrote to me.

Today I find it particularly important to always try to maintain the balance, to continue to motivate myself, to overcome my weaker self and keep going. I try to avoid situations that will make me unhappy. I sometimes decline an invitation to a friend's party that many hearing people would attend because I know I would only be able to watch as the others happily chatted away. Nevertheless, I still like to be invited. The main reasons: 1. There is normally good food at parties. 2. Even if I really don't want to go, there is always the chance that I will experience something new or unexpected. Sometimes I say, "No, thanks". Sometimes I find it important to deliberately put myself in those situations as they help me to (re)define my boundaries and give me the kick up the arse that I need. I actively try to stay healthy mentally, by doing this I avoid slipping into spells of depression or longer-term depression. Because if I do slip downwards, my body slides with me, and pulling yourself out of a downward spiral is anything but easy.

But it is definitely possible - it is just much easier if you catch yourself before you start to fall. I have started to keep a 'Happy Jar' since last year which is where I collect Post-its. When I am feeling particularly good about any kind of situation or when I had to laugh heartily about something, I write it down and put the slip of paper in the jar; when I am not feeling so good, I take the slip of paper out. Thank you for the idea someone on the internet!

In the rehab clinic, with my mind on 'going home', I began to feel a bit better again. I marked the day that I would be checking out of the hotel on the calendar weeks in advance. Not much longer …

Years later I learnt that the mind and body are connected; if one is affected so the other will be affected too. During the time that I was in a bad way, physically, the last thing that would have come to mind (if anything did at all) would have been to write a poem. As I began to improve after two years of hard struggle, and I found out that a friend of mine in the same boat was going downhill physically, I tried to give her courage.

Mind and body

I'm writing to you not because I should
But because I want to
Although I've long wanted to
I still remained mute

One stanza is enough for me
Because I'm doing really well
The next few lines are for you
I hope they give you courage

I'm not so sure
How you are today
All I know is that this past year
Everything has changed

Physically you're struggling
Yet mentally you're strong
You are known for being fit and cheerful
We all love this about you

And no one can take it from you
It is a part of you
Perhaps it's hard to see right now
Just how special you are

And as you fully know
Our body is a power
And part of that's the mind
Together they are marvellous

And when your body suffers
Things go more and more downhill
The mind loses courage
And energy drains away

In times where the body suffers
And the mind is drained as well
It can't be avoided
That it defends itself only very little.

And yet look upon the time
In which your mind has grown
it is far too strong
For it to leave you behind

The flames that burn inside you
Are called Patience and Hope
And together they will both
Chase the turmoil away

For this New Year I'm sending to you
Confidence and strength
You'll soon be back
You'll soon make it through.

Original:

Mind and body

Ich schreibe dir nicht weil ich sollte
Sondern weil ich will
Obwohl ichs schon länger wollte
War ich doch etwas still

Eine Strophe reicht für mich
Denn mir gehts viel zu gut
Die nächsten Zeilen sind für dich
Ich hoff sie machen Mut

Mir ist wenig klar,
wies dir grad so geht
nur weiß ich das sich im letzten Jahr
sich vieles hat gedreht

Physisch ging's für dich hinunter
Mental bist du jedoch stark
Man kennt dich nur so fit und munter
Was man an dir besonders mag

Und das kann dir niemand nehmen
Denn das ist dein Naturell
Vielleicht gerade schwierig wahrzunehmen
Doch du bist ganz speziell!

Und wie du sicher weißt
Ist unser Körper eine Kraft
Doch dazu gehört der Geist
Zusammen sind sie fabelhaft

Und gehts dem Körper nicht so gut,
geht es immer mehr bergab
fehlt auch dem Geiste etwas Mut
und die Kraft wird knapp

In Zeiten wo der Körper leidet
Und auch am Geiste zehrt
Lässt sich nicht vermeiden,
dass er sich wenig wehrt

Doch betrachtest du die Zeit
In der du den Geist hast wachsen lassen
Wär es noch viel zu weit
Für ihn, um dich zu verlassen.

Die Flamme welche in dir glimmt
Heißt Hoffnung und Geduld
Und zusammen ganz bestimmt
Entfliehn sie dem Tumult.

Ich sende dir fürs neue Jahr
Zuversicht und Kraft
Bald bist du wieder da,
bald hast du es geschafft!

Home!

On the last day of rehab my parents introduced me to Nadine who would be continuing my occupational therapy at home. I didn't know how lucky I was and it was just at the moment that she walked into my room on the ward that I asked sharply: "Who is she then, and what does she want?"

After I was finally allowed home my parents faced a huge challenge. Preparations had been made, of which I had had no idea. I wasn't interested, anyway. There was only: "Home!" Our house was anything but fully accessible for a person in my position, starting with the steep driveway and the steps at the doorway. I was to have my bedroom upstairs - there was simply no way for it to be downstairs. A lot of equipment was required: Suction equipment for the tracheal cannula in case something got into my lungs again. Oxygen tanks in case I became short of breath. Packets full of artificial food that were to be pumped into my stomach - we spent a long time trying various different brands until we found one that didn't make me feel sick. My father took over showering me. I felt like a baby and complained constantly.

Everything had been thought about with love: a baby monitor for communication when I needed something upstairs, even a camera for supervision - which was something I absolutely did not want to get used to. I also had a rattle next to my bed and an even louder set of hand clappers which were actually meant for football fans. The national colours of the hand clappers? Italian! After a few months of my parents having their hands completely full with everything we employed a nursing service. And that is how we met Kay, who looked after me with unbelievable care, who could communicate with me really quickly using the finger alphabet and sign language and who withstood my often terrible moods brilliantly. Various helpers looked after me on a daily basis and took me to physiotherapy, to see the psychologist and even on little outings here and there. They helped with the everyday things and saw to the medicinal things such as changing the tracheal cannula, and helping me get my trousers down when I needed to go to the toilet as I needed both my hands to hold myself steady. They were all essentially strangers to me. Some were rougher than others but they were always conscientious. In rehab I had sometimes used a walker to get around. At home I took the wrong approach, I thought that nothing would ever get any better, and I resigned myself to my fate and only used a wheelchair. Why should I struggle to walk when it was much more comfortable to stay seated to move around? I only continued going to physiotherapy because I thought I had to, until one day I requested to finish having sessions. I had lost faith. I wrote resignedly:

"It doesn't mean that nothing is happening, just that it is happening unbearably slowly. And when you see yourself every day, then it looks like as if nothing is happening and if it's in the back of your mind that it could all go downhill … it is not a nice feeling. Anyway, at the minute things are stable."

So that it didn't get worse, however, I used a MOTOmed at home - an exercise system for wheelchair users - to keep my legs moving. Nevertheless, it annoyed me. I didn't want to spend my whole life training my legs when they weren't going to be able to do anything anyway. I wanted to be able to enjoy it. My psychologist talked of accepting the wheelchair. It turned my stomach - that thing simply did not belong to me. And it was the person who pushed me around it in that got to call the shots anyway. I couldn't change anything about it, or so I believed. At that time, when I still wasn't ready, I wrote:

"So of course, I am very sad about my losses, above all the ability to walk and eat. I know how life should be, and that makes it so difficult. In some moments I watch 'normal people' and feel like I could burst with envy: Man! Why isn't my life like theirs? But: Life must go on. Somehow you cling to life. I become really angry when I see how people throw it away for no good reason, or when people risk their health. I could say it a thousand times: Life is built on health - it is the be-all and end-all. Believe me and learn to look after your health!"

Since then, I have come to realise that everyone has their own problems and priorities, and I can understand if something else is more important to someone else. In my opinion, someone who does not feel well - for whatever reason - has a real problem that is just as bad or possibly worse. What I have to deal with, compared to them - is that not terrible? Who is it that decides that what I feel is terrible? The Dalai Lama has said: "Pain is unavoidable, suffering is optional," And there is someone who has suffered! He has had it much worse that I have. Please, no pity where it is not needed.

In my opinion, many people have no idea what their lives are worth. I do. The things I complain about have become much less. But that is completely OK. I think everyone has a right to deal with and approach their own problems in a completely individual way; it is a matter of perspective. A big positive that I was able to see, and that I continue to, is how people in my presence become aware of something better. The load that others carry sometimes becomes visibly lighter for them. It is a source of great happiness for me if I can, through my own mere existence, alleviate the suffering of someone else. He who helps others, above all, helps himself. And I don't have to do anything to achieve that.

As a result my health is naturally even more valuable to me; now that I have lost part of it. When they meet me, I often think, I can see others thinking: "Just how can you live like this and still be happy?", some even say it out loud. "You could be, as well!" I reply. I mean it in earnest … but it doesn't get taken seriously. It is incomprehensible from the perspective of a healthy person, for example. That much is obvious. Before I was in this position myself, I would probably also have thought: "I'll never be able to manage it!" Today, my life is completely normal for me and I always wish that others could see that. But they often just see suffering where there is none. I take this stigma on the chin. When I am not being held back by others, life is great.

Comeback

In spite of everything we set ourselves one goal: more independence. We took it in small steps. The cannulas were less often closed by the little balloon on the inside of the air pipe, designed to prevent food getting into my lungs, meaning that my upper airway was more often clear and I could breathe naturally and talk. The ongoing nausea had almost completely disappeared and some of my devoted carers were learning sign language. My wonderful hearing therapist, who had helped me through the first year of my deafness and the painful process of coming to terms with my new, changed identity, took it upon herself to set up a signing course for Nadine, my occupational therapist, and Nicola, a lovely carer from the neighbourhood. The wheelchair was exchanged for an electric one, so that I could decide for myself where I wanted to go. That gave me a lot of freedom. I went to the funfair and drove myself round and round in circles - literally – just for fun. It was a great step in the right direction, if only a metaphorical one. Old friends like Sebbo from my primary school came to see me and we played poker. We had lost touch after leaving school but now he is a good friend. Considering that most NF2 sufferers find that the friendships from their pre–deafness days don't survive, I find it really special when I can reconnect with old companions.

Around that time I started on a new and promising treatment that involved travelling to Hamburg; it was then that my progress towards mobility really started. One day I just got up from my wheelchair. I started physiotherapy again, enthusiastically this time, because now I wanted to do it. At the same time we moved to a wheelchair-accessible flat in town. My mother and I still miss the garden and the fireplace of the old house but that's peanuts compared with the opportunities the new flat has given me. Suddenly I could go into town on my own in my electric wheelchair on the tram; as time went on I began to go on longer trips and more frequently.

In the times when I had been unmotivated, adrift in lethargy, and had allowed myself to be pushed everywhere, my brother used to say: "I can't understand why you don't do something." It made me angry and upset that he wasn't on my side and didn't support me in my decisions. But then I began to understand him. A lightbulb moment. In retrospect, I can see that several positive factors came together at that time, the antibody treatment being the most important. This required a trip on the fast long distance train to Hamburg with my two guardian angels, Nadine and Nicola, and of course a detour through Hamburg's famous red light district...

But I also know that it was due to my own efforts that things started to improve around that time. Thanks to months of swallowing practice I can now appreciate every bite of food. My precious treasure, the wonderful Nadine, came to our home every week and practised patiently with me until the feeding tube and the cannula could be removed. Even though I still had some problems with chewing and swallowing we had, together, reached our goal. It took about 18 months of gradually reducing the amount of feeding via the tube until my chewing muscles gained enough strength for it to be removed. We started cooking soups together in the new flat and gradually I succeeded in eating enough to keep my weight steady. When I look back on that time I feel proud and grateful. Now I sometimes make soups myself, using the cookery book I bought at the time, as part of my independence project. There should be more people in the world like Nadine. Without her determination, encouragement and, especially, empathy I don't think I would have reached this level. She told me later that she tells my story to encourage other patients who are overwhelmed by their illness. She uses me as an object lesson to prove that even in a miserable and seemingly impossible situation, perserving and fighting is always worth it. She enjoyed working with me; it was a win-win situation and who doesn't like those?

More and more often in restaurants these days I order things that I know will be difficult for me to eat and which I probably won't manage. I usually arrange a snack for a couple of hours later in case I haven't been able to eat enough. Pushing the limits like this gives me some longed-for freedom. And anyway, I have always been stubborn.

Various factors, then, coincided to bring me to the point where I felt I had turned a corner. I began to take back control of my life. Was it Nadine? Was it my brother, Pascal, who was constantly nagging me? The new electric wheelchair that I could control myself? The new flat and the independence it gave me? Or my parents, especially my father who acted as my secretary and supported me in all sorts of ways – interpreting here, taking on the battles with the health insurance there, explaining yet again why I needed an electric wheelchair. The health insurance was not interested in the improved quality of life it would bring me; we had to prove that the carers couldn't push the wheelchair up the steep ramp at the entrance to our house. He knew the right language and the right ploys to use and he still uses them to cut a path through the jungle that is German bureaucracy. Then, at some point, my new treatment in Hamburg began. We set off with our bags full of hope that the growth of the tumours would at least be halted. The tumours in my head were critical by now, nobody wanted an operation, so it was worth a try... I was lucky; it was a success, but more of that later.

I think all of these actions re-awakened the fighter in me. I took things into my own hands again and from then on events seemed to progress automatically. Before that I had allowed myself to lie down and submit to what was happening – in other words I acted the layabout – but not any more. I recognised that a lot more was possible and I started to work towards achieving it, quite simply because I wanted to. Where there's a will, there's a way! I still believe in that saying and I am always quoting it. Also, that nothing comes from nothing; a lot of people used to say that to me in the time before my new positive attitude. Nothing was going to happen until I wanted it to happen. And now I did.

For a long time I had thought that the main reason for my inability to walk was my loss of balance caused by the severed auditory nerves. In fact, I now realised, it was my weakened muscles. After my operation I had been immobile in bed in intensive care for six weeks. That was followed by four months in rehab where I walked for only five minutes a day with the walking frame. So I was lying or sitting for 98% of every day. Admittedly my balance was still poor and perhaps if it had improved more quickly I would have been able to start walking sooner. But my muscles had shrunk and five minutes of exercise was the most I could manage, only then, with extreme effort.

It was not fun and I wasn't making any progress. I thought that if my balance was destroyed it was destroyed, and no amount of exercise would make any difference. But I was wrong! I now know that, unlike with hearing, the sense of balance can be relearned, with intense practice. Do I regret the time I lost? No. I needed that time and I am pleased that in the end I still managed to achieve something. Better late than never!

I was still in the wheelchair in our old house but in the new flat I vowed that I would walk, with the aid of a walker, all the time. I knew I didn't belong in a wheelchair; it wasn't my destiny. I wanted to be rid of it, so I exercised every day, and every other day I went to the physiotherapy gym and used the equipment there to try to build up my muscles to enable me to compensate, at least partially, for my loss of balance. At these sessions, two or three times a week, Carmen and Marcel helped me to achieve the miracle of getting on my feet again. Years later Marcel is still patiently supporting me towards my new goals. We have even become friends. Sometimes we see each other more, sometimes less, but he has become an important part of my life.

Anne, who has kept in touch with me through regular meetings since my time in Munich says he saw a completely different person in the rehabilitation centre – face contorted, slumped in a wheelchair, depressive... I wrote to him when things were getting better - 'I am going to get out of this wheelchair, I will make sure of that!' I was ready for action and full of energy; I hadn't felt so well for a long time and was determined that things were going to change. And they did.

I no longer worry about what NF2 will do to me next – I

know that whatever happens I will always be able to pick myself up again. NF2 is like a force constantly trying to push me down, it is up to me to fight it. It will always be like this but life is too short to give up on. Only I can decide the way I am heading. I finally realised that about two years after the second, serious operation – things just don't have to be like this. I was determined to get my independence back and, step by step, I did everything I could to achieve it. The feeding tube was removed from my stomach following a long period of sustained practice. Then the hole in my throat for the breathing tube was closed. I took up Spanish again via an online course - I knew it would be difficult, but not impossible, as I had discovered when I started Spanish at Southampton University before my operation. I just followed my instinct and found my way as I went along – and it was surprisingly simple. At home my two carers finally left, and I started going out on my own to prove to my parents that I could manage. I was starting to think about moving out and even eventually of fulfilling my goal of living in England. I had already had a taste of student life there. Suddenly this goal didn't feel so remote or absurd; it was an idea to be taken seriously. Anything was possible now. But, as always, it had to be one step at a time. Independence remained the first goal and I was getting there.

Progress happened gradually but by now it was consistently positive. Step by step I mastered each stage, set myself new goals, met Laura on the internet, fell in love a bit, she visited... I wrote this poem for her:

Grieving desire

I wake up, a new day will begin
I'm looking at my watch and almost start to grin
I turn around, staring at the wall,
I start to think "I really have it all!"

But then I realise something's missing:
Your tender skin, your lovely kissing
You touching me, your body-smell
Your hands in mine, it's really hard to tell!

When you blow air into my face
I don't want to be in any other place
But in your arms, next to you.
It feels like when a dream comes true...

When you put your arms around mine
When you gave me grins of sunshine
When you looked into my eyes
It was really hard to disguise
My happiness, your pleasure, our love?

But this would be my last attempt to have a relationship online. I am sure I could meet more people online who would
be prepared to get to know me without prejudice, but for me,
meeting someone new has to happen naturally, without the
computer. Of course an easy option for me would be to with-
draw into the virtual world. It certainly offers some advantages, particularly in communication. But I have noticed that

the more time I spend in front of the screen the more unhappy I feel. Strangely, it makes me feel lonely. So I have decided that this is not a route I want to take. I would rather try my luck as David facing Goliath on the battlefield of everyday life. It is hard not to lose my courage when society with its prejudices constantly chips away at it and treats me as if I'm incapable. But as I am re-building my life in the environment where I grew up, I feel confident that I need not lose touch with this familiar world. I have even invited a few of my old friends to informal weekly signing lessons, with me as teacher. Another win-win situation. Aren't these great?

One day a letter dropped through the letterbox from Southampton University. Although I had interrupted my first year there in order to have an operation, I was still registered as a student. How were things now? Had I recovered? This was unexpected – but why not? Here was another target to aim for. There were two months before the beginning of the next term, time enough to work on my independence and to reach the goal of getting out of my wheelchair. More motivation, more goals, more incentives.

As I said, the antibody therapy played an important part in this general improvement. I had been travelling to Hamburg with my carers every two weeks for my Avastin infusion. This is actually a cancer drug but an American researcher into NF2 discovered that it also works against NF2 brain tumours aswell. This occurs by inhibiting the blood supply to the tumours in the head. As a result the tumours have even been observed to shrink. Once we had established that I could tolerate the drug I was able to continue the treatment in Wurzburg. I only had to visit Hamburg once every three months to monitor my progress and agree on the next stage with the Professor there.

Meanwhile, as I had enrolled on an online course to keep my Spanish going, I would pack my books and set off in my electric wheelchair to the tram stop, take the tram into town and sit in my favourite café learning my Spanish. My mobile was vibrating in my pocket. I took it out and checked the screen: nothing. Probably only my stomach – or a fart! Not too loud, I hope.

CH4 (Methane)

Just imagine you are with someone,
in a small room.
oh no, there is trapped air in your tummy,
and not even just a little.

The air wants out, and that fast,
what a massive shituation.
so in a moment, while undistracted,
you just let one slip. hope that nothing could be heard,
and indeed there is no comment (thank god!).

Relieved you are in two ways
the air is out, there was no noise
but the other person grins,
so you start to suspect …
'he couldn't have…? It was quiet!'
and then he opens the window.

Original:

CH4 (Methan)

Stell dir vor du bist zu zweit,
in einer kleinen Räumlichkeit.
Oh nein, da ist luft im bauch,
und nicht grade wenig auch.

Die will raus und zwar schnell,
ein riesen scheiß Szenario gell?!
In einem Moment ganz ungestört,
lässt also einen zischen.
Hoffst und bangst dass man nichts hört,
Kommentar tust du vermissen (Gott sei Dank!).

Erleichtert bist du zweierlei:
die Luft ist raus, man hörte nichts,
der And're doch grinst heftig fei,
so kommt dir ein Verdacht.
Er kann doch nicht … es war doch still?
Und schon hat er das Fenster aufgemacht.

Land of my dreams?

With the online course nearly completed, I had only one goal in my head: going back to Southampton. I made all the necessary arrangements with the people at the university for support with communication, accommodation etc. There were discussions between my parents, my doctors and me about how to continue the Avastin treatment. My parents were thoroughly supportive of my plans.

My belongings were sent in a trunk to Southampton; some of my things were still there, stored with friends, from when I left to have the operation and didn't return.

I checked in my electric wheelchair with my suitcase, and from London I took a coach to Southampton. As soon as I arrived at my hall of residence I made a pact with myself that I would try to get by without using the wheelchair. That worked well and I only needed to use it outside. I can't remember how it happened, but I didn't hit it off with one of my flatmates and the hall of residence didn't have a canteen (I don't like cooking for one); so eventually I moved to the hall I had lived in the three years before. I still knew some people from the three months I had lived there before my operation and they helped me with the move to the new, old room.

People with special needs at university in England have all the expenses arising from their disability paid for. So I was always able to take a taxi if a lecture was on a different campus or I used my electric wheelchair on the rare occasions when it wasn't raining.

An advantage of the old hall of residence was that it was right next to the Faculty of Languages. So I didn't have to go far, after a while I tried to get there equipped only with my two walking sticks. I could now manage to walk to the café on my campus, including going up a couple of steps. This opened up new possibilities. Once I even managed to walk across the busy central campus, with professors and students rushing to and fro. Man, was that an experience, to be there without my wheelchair for the first time. And no-one noticed; because it looked so natural. It was wonderful. New opportunities, new horizons, new prospects.

At first I flew back to Hamburg from Gatwick every three weeks for my Avastin infusion, but later I was able to have it at the NF2 Centre in Oxford. I enjoyed my first year at university and it passed quickly, with the wonderful Wendy, the NF2 nurse. The whole team of the NF2 unit were simply smashing. Although it was not without some disappointments. Even though I searched, I found no-one in the university who knew sign language. The door to my room was always open but few people dropped by. One or two did take up the invitation and that made me happy. We would cook together, play Fifa or I would be invited to watch a film. Once I even went to one of the numerous parties that happened in Southampton. But to most of the students I was just "the strange bloke who can't hear." We never really got to know each other and that didn't matter to me. Well, not much. It meant that I had to face up to my solitude.

I expressed this and other failed expectations of my life in England in a poem:

Nowhere

Before I came, I thought
this would be my home
this is what I sought
this is where I belong

Full of expectation
I told friends how it would be
With all my imagination
I was sure of what I'd see

With every passing day
though, I feel less certain, and
that this is far away
from my self-promised land

Yet people are the same
It's just another way of living
It's just a different game
Just as unforgiving

What are people looking for?
Why is all so complicated?
Why do we just want more and more?
This greed just makes us separated:

From human values deep within
Though our heart is just as real
We don't have to win
We just have to feel.

However, I am glad that I took the step of studying in England and I don't regret a second of my life there, although I must admit I was sometimes disappointed. Even here it was a constant battle to re-integrate into the normal world I had left behind. Or perhaps I just wasn't ready to let go of the beloved world I had once known, new environment I had created for myself.

Resuming my studies, it wasn't long before I exchanged the standard note-taking assistant who sat next to me in lectures in favour of a system of remote captioning via the internet; someone would listen to the lectures using Skype, speed type the content into a website which I would then access and read on my laptop. Only later did I discover that I was the first deaf student to use this system in England. Since then I believe it has has also been used standard at other universities. And all because Steve, a deafened man whom I met during my search for other deafened people, mentioned the system to me one day in a café in Southampton when I said I wasn't happy with my note-takers. Little did I know then, how these two words (Remote Captioning) would change my life at university. I went straight back to my room and searched the internet and found out about this technology. I was so excited; my heart was racing, my eyes were shining as I realised how perfectly this system could support me in my studies. I wasn't disappointed. I wrote an email enquiring whether it would be practical in my situation, little expecting what awaited me. Two weeks later my little revolution happened and I began to feel I was flying. Beth, the manager who set up the system, was always ready to listen to my ideas and together we perfected the practical arrangements in the classes, the application of the technology and we made the teaching staff aware of the system so that they could support me too. They were all fascinated by it. I wished I had three times as many lectures and tutorials! Win-win? Even more than that.

Buried in essays on 'The future of English' for linguistics, working through the history of Spanish, writing a persuasive speech as an exercise in rhetorical English, with these and many other new experiences the first year at university passed. I was standing on my own two feet again. My health had stabilised and I felt better than ever as I set off for Wurzburg to join my family for the summer holiday. I was already looking forward to the second year, all the more so because just before the end of the first year I had finally met somebody who knew sign language; Rob would become my closest friend at university.

The summit

Soon after we met, we started giving signing lessons together. I had already tried to teach a few people German sign language, but from now on it would have to be British Sign Language (BSL). I learned it by teaching it.

In our second year we organised SignSoc and soon we had 200 members, although of course only about a quarter, or less, of them came regularly. SignSoc became very important to me. It helped me out of my loneliness by enabling me to build up a community and provided contact, if only superficial, with other people (an added bonus – mainly girls.) In the second year I also joined the Spanish Society. A trip to Barcelona was advertised and I signed up like a shot. At the same time my balance was improving so much that after a few months I could walk completely unaided. Armed with walking sticks and a Frisbee, I found myself walking past the very spot where, two years earlier on a trip with my brother, I had taken my first steps out of the wheelchair in public. No-one was aware of this except me as I hurried along with the others, a large grin etched across my face. On an outing somewhere one evening with the group I did a short hop and fell flat on my face. Never mind, there was no damage done. Or so I thought; by four o'clock in the morning I could no longer endure the pain in my leg and I had to ask my room neighbours to call an ambulance. After waiting for hours at A & E in the end I was given some pain killers. This miraculous cure must have done the trick because eventually the pain subsided. Back in Southampton I acted as referee for our really lousy Modern

Languages football team (InterMilanguages) where fun came before skill. There were regular games against other teams, such as the Biology team (Ajax Trees), the Chemistry team (Special Brew), Philosophy (River Plato), or the Mexican Society who thrashed us so mercilessly that I lost count of the goals. I carried my red and yellow cards and wore a bright yellow shirt on which I had written: You can't argue with me!

In my second year I found a place where I really felt at home. The 'Art House,' a not-for-profit community café which served one thing above all else: love. There were 'Language Cafés' here, like the weekly 'Sign Language Café' led by Tony, the wonderful, funny, deaf guy; workshops on all sorts of things: drawing, creative writing and street music; a lot of humour and there were always art displays. Delicious food, lovingly prepared, was served by volunteer helpers. For a while, when I was fit, I volunteered in the café, and enjoyed doing it. Every time I walked in it was like entering another world. This was where many of my poems were written, inspired by the sense of community and the congenial atmosphere. Such as this one …

The shower

Outside it's dark and getting cold
it's grey and rain is biting.
Clouds move wildly, fighting.
The day's about to fold.

I was going to go out
so I stepped outside the door.

Suddenly I didn't want to anymore
and thought "what's this about?"

The weather wouldn't rest
so I hurried back inside.
Surrendered to the night
felt feeble and depressed.

Saw curtains slightly blowing
and also felt a breeze.
Heard windows hit by trees
the force of all was growing.

I longed for warmth instead
so took a steaming shower.
By that, regained my power
and escaped the threat.

My time in Southampton, certainly from the beginning of
my second year, was turning out to be the happiest of my life,
and I now knew that my decision to come here had been the
right one.

Thanks to a device called a text phone, which converted
speech into text on a screen, I was able to use the telephone
again. I also had a television in my room which had subtitles
for all programmes. What a luxury to be able to sit down, turn
on the TV and watch whatever was on. No more checking in
advance to see whether the programme had subtitles. I felt
much less handicapped than I had in Germany. I wonder why

things are much less well set up for disabled people in Germany than they are in England. People in England complain about the quality of live subtitles. I was grateful to have them at all. I had always thought that Germany was better when it came to technology, but the standard of subtitling there is a disgrace. We hearing-impaired people are being deliberately deprived of our right to information and culture. After seeing how good it is in England I just don't watch television any more in Germany – and I feel let down. I can't accept anything less than 100% now. I would love to sit down with my father and watch an interesting programme with him. No subtitles? I leave the room fuming.

At university, for the first time in years, I began to find myself having to choose between two clashing events, both of which I was interested in. Okay, not a good situation per se but it definitely felt good to be in it.

Of course I still had to initiate things myself; people in England were also hesitant in communicating with me, but that's quite normal when people are confronted with something like deafness for the first time. I am patient. A patient patient.

But, above all, I just loved being at university with its interesting lectures and seminars. In Spanish, the remote captioning allowed me to read the lectures on my screen in real time – in Spanish. I never again wanted to miss a lecture and with this support I felt on top of my studies. I really liked the student body at the university. Southampton has around 20,000 students of whom about 8,000 are foreigners. I met people from France, Spain, Italy, Greece, Cyprus, Turkey, Poland, Germany, Austria, the Netherlands, Wales, England, Norway, Sweden, India, Pakistan, China/Hong Kong, Malaysia, Trinidad and Tobago, USA, Mexico, Australia, Ghana, Libya – all in just a couple of months.

So, all in all, things were going well for me. But still, I couldn't help witnessing how quickly friendships developed between students in the hall of residence. I had got used to this sort of situation by now – watching others having fun while I was left behind. Sometimes friendships seemed to start on the same route for me, they just went much more slowly and were more likely to fail. Sometimes I make the decision not to be too open with people; this self-mindfulness means that it's not easy for people to get to know my true self. It is only after the first hurdle has been cleared that friendships really become worthwhile. It is too upsetting to be left standing in the rain after telling someone my whole story too soon.

Everywhere in the hall of residence small groups of students were always standing around. If I tried to join one I would find myself in the middle of a group of hearing people all chatting to each other. Standing there, I quickly realised I had no idea what is going on – what they were talking about, what they were laughing about. It made me feel like a dog and I try not to put myself in that situation now. If I do sometimes end up in that sort of situation by accident, in the dining hall for instance, there is only one thing I can do; explain politely and escape before things get too difficult.

But I didn't pay too much attention to these things. Life had taken a giant leap forwards and I was living it to the full. Meditation helped to bring me down to earth. But I had never felt so happy and I was happy that my friends and family at home were happy, too. What do you call a vicious circle of happiness?

Intermission

It was a grey day in Southampton just before Christmas and my watch strap had broken. I wanted to get it mended so I set off in my car, unsuspecting, to the shopping centre. I had got the car thanks to a UK association called Motability, I gave them part of my disability allowance and received the car in return. And it gave me more – no, much, much more mobility and hence an improved quality of life.

Fucking hell – it's busy here, I thought, as I parked the car, got out the walker and started off towards the repair shop in the shopping centre. Crowds of people were rushing to and fro, flying past me, almost tripping over my walker; they were acting like like zombies, I thought, victims of the consumer society. I made some progress, thanks to one or two people who were a little less inconsiderate, but I could see that before long my walker and I would be swallowed up by the surging masses, all determined to buy their presents. After a while I gave up, turned round and battled my way in the opposite direction to the Art House café where I sank into a sofa with a hot chocolate. I shook my head in despair and vented my feelings about consumerism in the way I know best.

Black or White

Buy this, buy that,
we'll even tell you what to eat
and you decide if it's good or bad.
Now that's service at your feet.

No need to think
we're doing it for you,
you only have to blink
for product number two.

Come and play our game!
You can only win, we promise you!
All the prizes are the same,
and there's a bonus, too!

What, you aren't satisfied?
Not happy with your choice?
But you could go for wrong or right!
Of course we heard your voice!

But we won't tell you this:

We actually don't care,
we have your money now,
and of course it was fair!
You have made a vow!

By letting you choose
between black or white
you actually lose
without the need to fight!

We're clever dicks!
Pretend you're in control
we're pretty chicks,
and this is how we roll!

Arriving in Germany in the Easter vacation for a minor operation to remove some irritating skin tumours, I was looking
forward to the spring and I captured the feeling in a poem:

The Sun

When winter slowly fades away
and after months of perma-night
it to another power gives its way
to a most suppressed delight.

It summons the respect which it earns,
for once its value we do cherish.
It is then that human learns
and feels that discontent will perish.

The first rays on the balcony
relieve the heart and lift one's spirit,
from winter's gnawing agony –
a fire in the soul is lit.

At once we sense its woken passion
the warmth gives us a spell of joy.
We desire for it to become the fashion
and want it to cease the winter's ploy.

Just before leaving for Germany I had been at an NF2 conference in Manchester and I had been moved to see so many specialists dedicating themselves to researching and working on this illness. Here, for the first time, I noticed that I was less steady as I walked with my sticks to the hotel. Because of the planned operation my Avastin therapy had been suspended for three months.

Back in Germany I went to visit my brother at the village of Tempelhof, an alternative community in the countryside in Baden-Württemberg where people live a sustainable, ecological and, above all, communal life. While I was there I kicked a ball around for the first time for years, not minding that I looked like a giant toddler!

It was about this time that I came across Marshall Rosenberg and his wonderful theory of 'Nonviolent Communication' (NVC), which I read about in depth, fascinated. This philosophy of life, and model for the way we communicate with our fellow humans, changed my life. It was thanks to this that I discovered the needs in me which govern my emotions and cause me to react angrily in certain situations, or allow other people to make me sad, and I understood the emotional power of simple words like "always," and "everyone." I find it bloody hard to live by this philosophy of communication but I am glad to have discovered it and I would recommend everyone to find out about it. It certainly enriched my life.

The planned operation took place in the week following my visit to Tempelhof and the two skin tumours were removed with no complications. The only problem that emerged was that I needed another, more serious, operation to save my sight which was being threatened by an apparent build-up of pressure in the brain. The doctors said it was necessary to reduce the pressure by implanting a tube in the brain through which the excess fluid could drain away. Called a shunt, this tube would ensure that the pressure was regulated. It certainly needed to be done, but it would further extend the time I was without Avastin.

At one of the annual meetings of NF2ers in the village of Mücke, in Hessia, I met Annemarie. I was quickly convinced that I had met the woman of my dreams. However, I decided to get to know her better. Sadly her heart was engaged elsewhere and my approaches were in vain and eventually I had to accept that. But I have never again found such a special person, such a kindred spirit, such a close friend as her. We still keep in touch and are very close friends. Looking back on it, meeting Annemarie was the highlight of my life.

I had now been without Avastin for several months. The operation took place shortly after the Mücke gathering, and was successful, but I had already become aware of a marked deterioration in my mobility and this increased after the operation. Another MRI scan confirmed what we already knew from the worsening symptoms: that while the Avastin treatment had been stopped the tumours had grown rapidly and had reached, or even exceeded, the size they had been before. The immediate effect for me was that my progress was put into reverse. I was slipping backwards, losing all the improvements

I had fought so hard to achieve. From walking independently with my walking sticks I was now back in the wheelchair. The palsy in my face was worse and now I was also losing the feeling in my hands and legs. After 6 months without the treatment I was not only back in a wheelchair but I was close to needing carers again. But then I started back on Avastin and I was full of hope that things would get back to how they had been before the interruption. I was very lucky; my condition did indeed gradually improve. It was summer 2012 and my father, my brother and I had planned a rafting holiday in Sweden. However, I was not well enough and, with heavy hearts, we had to cancel it. Instead, we devoted the summer to the project of getting me fit again – this was not how I had imagined the long summer months. With renewed determination, I resumed my regular visits to the physiotherapy gym with one aim: to walk again. And indeed after a couple of months, when the Avastin had taken effect and the tumours had begun to shrink, I found myself almost there; close to being able to walk without the walker. But it never got any better. The physiotherapy, the yoga and all the exercising had helped, but today I am still only almost there. I still can't walk without the walker, and I am not happy about it. I know it is all down to me … if only my muscles were stronger my walking would be more reliable. I am working on it …

The finish line

My last year at university was another good one. By now I felt more at home there and everything worked smoothly. Rob and I continued to teach our weekly BSL lessons and had a lot of fun. The other day we wanted to go to a gym in a different halls complex and he asked me: 'Shall we take the car or walk?' In response to this, my German brain thought: 'Ich muss meinen inneren Schweinehund bekämpfen,' and so we walked. Literally, it means: to fight my inner pig-dog. "What??", he asked. I tried to explain it: "Fight my inner devil?" – "ohhh!" Actually, it means to 'fight your weaker self.' So, take a situation where you have to force yourself to do something and in order to do it, you have to overcome your inner pig-dog, or in other words, laziness. I overcame my inner pig-dog when I chose to walk instead of taking the car. I find discussing these expressions in any language so exciting, it feels like a new discovery and it gets me every time, especially when the enthusiasm is shared. With polyglot Rob, this was standard and I enjoyed it very much. With Manar, from Libya, I got to meet another outstanding person. We were in the same Spanish class at the beginning and from then on kept practising together. She was humble, her attitude to work was admirable and I was also able to learn more about Islam and her culture. She also helped with setting up SignSoc and even taught classes with me. She was a very reliable partner.

I wrote my dissertation on the effects of acquired hearing loss and this was my favourite part of the whole degree. In the last year Ella came into my life. When she turned up in our signing class I couldn't take my eyes off her. Later it turned out that she was learning German - and also that she wasn't available. I loved making her laugh. Luckily we were both lingo-freaks and no well-worn pun of mine was too stupid for her. Somewhere I read: "To make her fall in love you have to make her laugh. But every time she laughs, I am the one who falls in love." And that's what happened. Sometimes just a look was enough. It's a miracle that she kept in touch with me – to this day we still write to each other. I often think back to the moment when I first saw her and Cupid's arrow struck. For me it just happened. For her, it seems it didn't. But that's OK. After all, she was taken! The important thing is that she would still be in my life. I wanted to pour out my heart to her, so I wrote her a poem. I didn't think she would want to have it then, so I just gave her the last verse as a parting gift when I left Southampton. Almost a year later, I showed her the whole poem and she was grateful to see it.

Well I never

When I saw you first time ever
I never knew before
I never was so sure
Well I never

Believed in love at first sight
Now I know you slightly better
After doubts and my foolish letter
I knew my instincts had been right

And yet there is no limit for
knowing you better and all the days
I wonder about you and your ways
I want to know you even more

For now our ways shall part
where to I do not know

Of one thing I am certain though
You shall remain forever in my heart

Just before the end of my degree there was another small
shock. A tumour on my back was beginning to press on my
spinal cord and needed to be removed. Paraplegia was on the
cards. I was worried that I would have to interrupt my studies
again, and so close to the finish line! But my trusted surgeon
worked a miracle and three days after the operation I was discharged; not long after that I found myself on the Costa del
Sol. My father and I treated ourselves to this unexpected trip
to celebrate the success of my operation.

Back in England I received my degree in the summer of 2014. My parents were there, filled with pride, as was my tutor and my lecturers in English and, especially, Spanish, all of whom had been with me for the whole three years. It seems they were not the only ones supporting me. I was told later that the whole hall burst into applause as I walked back to my place with my degree certificate. The cynical part of me thought: "It was only because you walk so slowly and they were bored."

Paty, from Mexico, who had heard me stammer my first words in Spanish, had been with me on my quest to be able to communicate with Spanish speaking people. This, after all, had always been my goal, as I had often reminded her - in emails in English instead of Spanish due to my laid-back attitude to work, or simple laziness. I wasn't interested in getting top marks or driving myself mad with revising and practising, I didn't mind what marks I got as long as I passed. And I managed that fairly easily. Well, not I - but we. Paty was always on my side. She was so good at adapting her teaching for me that I could follow everything without the rest of the class being held back. In one-to-one tutorials, especially in the first year, she would go through material again with me. Every time I left her room, I would turn back after a few steps, wag my finger at her and say: "Otra Cosa!" (And another thing ...), not only because there were so many things we could talk about but simply because I enjoyed it so much and didn't want to leave. There were so many tears when I left. I loved her typical Mexican warm-heartedness and I wanted to show her how grateful I was, so in my last year I wrote her a poem, my first in Spanish: Translation (non-rhyming, in order to maintain the meaning.)

Oh, and another Thing

Soon it will be over
this turbulent time
in my life and without
doubt I am glad.

However,
a part of me will be sad
My heart will weep a lot
Remembering all the doors you opened for me.

Through them I have grown,
And not only as a linguist
But also, it seems,
As a person, soul and spirit.

And all this was possible
Only with you
My incredible teacher number one
I never tire

For this reason, I have chosen not to cry
because it is all over,
but to smile instead
because it happened

Original:

Ay, Otra cosa!

Prontito marcará el fin
de un periodo turbulento
En mi vida y sin
duda me siento contento

no obstante
Una parte de mi estará triste
Mi corazon va a llorar bastante
Recordando las ventanas que me abriste

A través de ellas he crecido mucho
No solo lingüisticamente
Sino que como persona escucho
Con el alma y también la mente

Y esto ha sido posible
Solo contigo
Mi maestra numero uno increible
Nunca me fatigo

Por eso he elegido
que en vez de llorar
por lo que pasó
voy a sonreir en su lugar

I particularly loved my English classes with my fabulous teacher Mary. She always made sure that we (mostly international) students would enjoy the classes and learn something valuable about English at the same time. And she also frequently asked the others about our cultures and languages. So interesting! With Mary, I shared a love for the English language and our humour was similar, not to mention our love of cats. I got to visit hers in the lovely place where she lives after graduation.

Every student at Southampton University has a personal tutor assigned to them at the beginning of their course, here again I was very lucky. Adrian met me regularly and supported me through the whole course. I have seldom met anyone as enthusiastic as him, about his job, definitely about his students and not forgetting FC Union Berlin! He was always sensitive to me and my situation, helping me through the jungle of bureaucracy (yes, England has one too) allowing my year-abroad project to develop easily into a dissertation or getting me an extension for a piece of work without losing any marks.

The Disability Team, particularly Adam, with my assistance, organised my speech-to-text interpreters as well as Kathryn with accomodation-related things. Altogether, there was an ideal network in place for someone with special needs like me and I am so grateful to everyone involved for enabling me to have such a good time at university. I am reminded, once again, how much easier it is to row with a good team.

However, there was still no English NF2 community of the sort I had known in Germany; it had shocked and surprised me to discover this when I arrived in England. Still, I did make contact with some NF2 people and met Jessica, who was already trying to set up some sort of community. I told her about our annual 'Mücke gatherings' in Germany and perhaps this also encouraged her in her aspiration to set up the UK self-help group 'Can you Hear Us?' and I supported her as she built up the community. I got to know Jess better, a woman with a strong will, and soon we became good friends and perhaps a little more. In the summer of my last year the second gathering took place and it was, just as it was in Mücke, a unique experience to be in the company only of NF2 people for a weekend where all our disabilities were normal. And there were so many kindred spirits - the fabulous Paul, who supported me from behind for a game of pool, despite conjuring up strange images in the minds of those watching, Will who is always up for a laugh, Suzi, another admirable spirit with whom we turned the hotel lobby into a karaoke bar and so many more fantastic people. I expressed these feelings when in the company of other NF2 souls in a poem dedicated to all of them.

Home

In the course of the year
There are days
Where I feel alone here
In so many ways

And where is here, nobody knows
Especially not me
While my loneliness grows
And makes it hard to see:

That so many others feel the same
Day by day we feel caught
In the world from where we came
Where we once fought

Now we battle someplace else, everyone by himself
And every fruitful conversation
Feels like a trophy on a shelf
If we try hard we can overcome the situation

And some of these days we get together
All those stuck in the struggle throughout the year
The usual stones become the weight of a feather
And we are here...

In the place we dream of
Where magic happens, where we are ourselves
So much care and so much love
A million trophies for our shelves

And as the spirit gleams
My loneliness fades with energy recharged
Nothing is as it seems
My head held high, confidence enlarged

Thanks to my friends who show me
Where I am and that I'm never alone
That together we can be
In the place called home

In the same year, I was able to realise an idea that I had been thinking about; together with Annemarie and Ines from the German NF2 self-help group we formed a dream team and organised a seminar for our members. Topic: Non-violent communication. Place: Tempelhof. I enjoyed the preparations as much as the seminar itself and the whole experience was close to perfection.

The choice

In 2013 I celebrated the 10th anniversary of the start of my NF2 career with Matthias, who had been my bed neighbour in hospital in 2003. He had just been diagnosed too, and since then we have been firm friends. New Year's Eve 2013. Was it a cause for celebration or just a milestone? Was it negative? Well, a bit, certainly, but what's wrong with a bit of self-irony? We laughed about it – a great excuse for a party, anyway! A few others came as well and the gathering was entirely positive with a great atmosphere. I find that whenever a few NF2 people get together you can be sure of having a good time.

I am often asked whether I miss my hearing. Some deafened people answer with a clear "No." I haven't reached that point yet. Of course I miss it, every day. And yet I have noticed that as time goes by I am beginning to miss it less. Not being able to hear is becoming my new normality. But fundamentally, the loss is always there. "Doesn't it drive you mad, the endless silence?" people ask. Well, no. I can't change it so why get upset? This is how it is. I just have to make the best of it. Because of going deaf I have met a lot of great people, and recently I read these words by Martin Luther King: "Only in the darkness can you see the stars." So I try to think of how much I have grown through it, how much I have been able to learn and how much we have grown together as a family! Joining the German self-help group has almost given me another family, of sincere, kind-hearted people. Would I have met them if I had been healthy? At the beginning I remember saying "I feel as if I have been wrenched out of life." People who I thought were friends, moved away from me, except for a very few close ones. I lost my grip on the world I belonged to, and with it my identity, until only this small circle and my family were left ... But through this I have learned that quality in relationships is far more important than quantity, and this is something I remind myself of in all sorts of contexts. Within this reduced environment I feel particularly strongly supported and I cherish the precious relationships that I have. Not many friends stuck with me but I was very lucky; my family was always there for me. I take my hat off to anyone who has to get through the difficult early stages alone. Now my circle is made up of friends from my former life, D/deaf people, deafened people, and hearing people who know sign language - and even a few who don't, but they are the exception. I find it almost impossible to build a friendship with people when we have no common means of communicating and so most of the people in my circle know at least some sign language. I can only get anywhere with anyone else if they are prepared to adapt to my difficulties and learn some sign language. If not, they are as inaccessible to me as someone speaking a different language would be to a hearing person.

It's especially hard with my sister's children but they are too young to understand. Although I am not able to hear them learning to talk, my sister often lets me know some of the things I have missed. My three-year old niece, for example, announced something funny in kindergarten: In German 'Birne' means both a pear and a light bulb. And a spare bulb translates literally as a "spare pear" She meant she had a second pear with her in case anyone was hungry, but she what she said was: I have a spare bulb in case anyone gets hungry.

And the other niece, at about the same age, couldn't say the sound fr- and said s- instead, and on hearing a toilet flushing in the next compartment, said "Mummy, the sow has done a wee" (lady=Frau, sow=Sau). Anyway I'm glad we have the same sense of humour and my sister is also my best friend.

I generally enjoy challenges, they keep me motivated. I have also found it important to set myself goals that I can work towards, project by project. I read this quote recently: "The people who have the least to laugh about are often the ones with the most humour." I nod in agreement when I think of all the clowns around me; we NF2 people are definitely the funniest.

Of course there are lots of ways of coping with NF2 and different sufferers have found different ways. But I have found the way that seems to work for me. Humour is my mainstay, especially the self-irony mentioned earlier. The day I can no longer laugh at myself, it will be curtains for me. If only others would play along. But that's too much to ask. Anyway, I still laugh when people forget that I can't hear and send me a song, saying "You absolutely must listen to this!" … "That will be difficult", I answer, or some such comment, the person then realises and is mortally embarrassed. It's a shame that in chats, where this sort of thing usually happens, I can't see people's faces. I would die laughing, and I do so anyway at the mere thought of them.

But of course these little slips still leave their marks and there are many occasions when I get annoyed, for example when yet another email ends with "Just give me a call on this number:…" If someone does ring me on my mobile, I accept the call, say loudly in to the phone "Please text, I am deaf!" and hang up.

So, for me NF2 is not a disability but I am constantly disabled by it because of the widespread lack of awareness of it in society - and the government with its politics is not much better. Shouldn't someone be concerned about how people communicate with people without hearing? At the doctor's, after I have asked for the fifth time, in vain, for him to write down what he is saying and he simply talks on, I am overwhelmed with an impulse to just get up and leave. But I stay, and I have understood about two words and the rest of the conversation has gone to the winds. So I often have to take my parents with me as interpreters, because in Germany a doctor has no obligation to ensure successful communication with his patients, by providing an interpreter or a speech-to-text reporter. This is the sad state of affairs. I wonder what many people imagine it is like, not being able to hear? "Ah, but you can lip-read, can't you?" as if that's an alternative to hearing. If only it was so simple. "Ha-ha, good one!" I think. I want to say "Nope. Can you?" but I just say "Not really." Bam! "Oh right. Now what?" I can almost see written all over their faces in flashing lights. "Best if you can write it," I say, producing the pad and pencil I always carry, while they try to grasp that not hearing anything really means not hearing anything, find their imagination completely unequal to the task and write me off as someone who is unable to do anything. I can literally see them thinking: he can't do this, he can't do that, he can't do anything and he's stupid as well. Sometimes they simply don't understand what I have just said, they chatter on as if deafness were nothing and refuse to write anything down.

Sometimes I get away with just nodding sheepishly but then I have to remind myself "If you behave like that you will be the one who suffers."

In England the children in primary schools at least learn the finger alphabet. But in Germany ignorance of this is reflected in the whole of society, and if two people are using sign language in public they will definitely get funny looks, although some of these are just out of curiosity or fascination. That is fine but eventually it gets too much. We hearing impaired people quite often feel like something from another planet or an animal in the zoo.

As I have said, I try not to become bitter, but I am close to it. Frustration often still plays a big part. But I try to see every problem as a challenge. And after all, I still have a life, what a gift!

I didn't choose my fate. But I have chosen the way I cope with it and that is something I hold on to firmly. To live a happy life - isn't that what everyone strives for?

My particular burden has unlocked strengths and abilities in me and my family that we never knew existed. Just like in the story of the stone and the palm tree, I have turned my loss into gain. "How do you do it?" people ask. "I have no choice," I answer, and shrug my shoulders.

Standing at a window in Tempelhof in the late summer of 2014, I was momentarily transported to another place:

The Journey

At Tempelhof there is a room
where something special happens
slowly at first but then at the window
you find your mind bewitched

All at once swaying in the breeze
geraniums in full bloom
How beautiful they are
Oh how marvellous

You gaze across the hills and meadows
till your eye reaches the line of trees
a few giants with bare straight trunks
marking the edge of the forest

Out of the mix of many greens
the tallest giants reach for the blue sky
and charm me
The geraniums gently sway

but not from the breeze, no,
flitting from flower to flower
with fine wings beating quickly
a hummingbird in all its goodness

brings me gently back
to the place where I began
my transport of happiness
there where I can just let go.

Making sense

Some people complain that they can see no meaning to their existence and don't know what to do with their lives. I have discovered the meaning of my life; for while NF2 does not define my life it does give it a meaning. It is certainly never boring and it has made me the person I am today.

Besides, you only live once – even though that's a cliché. I live for the moment; so why would I mourn for what is lost? I have learned one thing – that you can't plan your life. That goes for NF2 sufferers and probably for everyone else as well. I don't make any plans for more than one or two years ahead, especially if there is a prospect of an operation. Who knows what this illness could still do to me? But just now that doesn't worry me – life is cool.

After the second major operation especially, I suffered a lot, and after existing for two years with 24/7 homecare, when things were finally starting to look up, I learned a lot more about the value of things I used to take for granted and of course about myself. Looking back, I am not sure anymore if I would have the same strength to endure the same situation again. Or do I have even more now that I have come through it? I don't know.

"So, now that the tumours have been removed, everything is OK, isn't it?" people ask, when they've heard my story. "If only!" I say. The tumours in my head are exactly the same size now as they were at the beginning, but at least I have had a few years without problems in that area. Apart from the time when I was without Avastin they haven't grown at all, and I am grateful for that. Of course, to begin with, my family and I were devastated when we had to start communicating with pencil and paper. These restrictions made my familiar world crumble. If anyone had told me then that one day I would be proud of myself, I'd have said they were crazy and shown them the door. Yet this is exactly what I say now to people who have just lost their hearing or been newly diagnosed with NF2. I think it motivates to think: "If he can do it, so can I."

After a few years my family and I came to understand the truth of the saying 'time is a great healer.' The time at the beginning was very hard and I think every NF2 sufferer has to go through it. But now, twelve years later, I would say that NF2 has breathed new life into me and, in a strange way, I am almost grateful for it.

Not that I find the illness itself a blessing – in fact it's a pain in the arse. But is has opened many doors for me. There is a Spanish word, "Suerte", which means both fortune and fate. Isn't that beautiful?

The Decision
But of course I still have to face reality and I constantly keep in mind what could still happen. These thoughts have been haunting me for years already, together with the oppressive knowledge that I have large tumours in my head that are pressing on my brain stem and can't be allowed to grow any further.

For years I have carried this difficult decision around with me wherever I go. Whether to act and have the operation, knowing that any operation can go wrong, knowing also that it could make things much better, and knowing too that all this weighing up of different possibilities doesn't help the situation at all.

My head teems with thousands of questions and I just can't imagine how it will turn out. Should I do it or not? Not a day goes past when I don't think about it, usually in the evening, when I am lying in bed. Then I ask myself the big question - although it can also strike without warning. "Wait a bit" I hear a voice whisper, but to wait until the right moment appears doesn't seem possible. What happens if my swallowing gets so much worse that I have to have a stomach tube again? What if...? "Let's wait and see then" I say to myself, feeling more light-hearted than I probably will ever again, and just give up thinking about it. My quality of life could either be greatly improved, or, like last time, it could get much worse and never get back again to how it was. Do I want to take that risk? But then we humans can only achieve things when we are not happy with our present situation – isn't that so? It is important for me that my family feels OK with the time I choose, for by now I have already made the decision to have the operation. At least for the moment. 51% in favour, 49% against. Figures variable. Things aren't helped by my mother's resistance to the idea of having surgery. Of course I can understand that. Why have an operation when I am so well? Think what they went through in 2008. Could they go through the whole thing again? "No," I say, "it won't be like that again," although I am not so sure myself. But in the end the decision whether to have another major operation or not is mine.

Although Avastin bought me several years of stability, I had known from the beginning that it wasn't a long-term solution. There is no data yet on the long-term effects of its use in treating NF2 sufferers, but it is known that it tends to stop being effective after about 6 or 7 years. That would be about now for me. Added to this there are the poisons it puts into the body and the increasing side-effects.

At the moment my NF2 is under control, which gives me the luxury of being able to make a decision at all. Should we wait until I am forced into making the decision when there is no longer any choice? We have seen what happens when the tumours grow by only a very small amount. Things go downhill rapidly; only if I am lucky will there be a chance of getting back to where I am now (by starting on Avastin again) – and even then the improvement can be uncertain and often only small. After starting on Avastin, when my tumours shrank a bit and were at their smallest, the months when I could walk unaided showed us that less pressure on my brain stem resulted in my sense of balance improving. My greatest wish now is to get back to that state. And the man who holds the key to this prospect is my surgeon, in whom I trust deeply.

Besides, I feel mentally ready now, physically almost so, and I can use the next couple of months to strengthen my body. The milestone of getting my degree has marked the close of an important phase of my life. And I have travelled.

The professor is an expert and I haven't heard of any other NF2 patient being in such a bad state as I was after the second operation in 2008. Of course I can't compare myself to anyone else, but what I know is that the operating procedures are much better now than they were seven years ago. Added to this, the professor himself is on good form now, the chance may not come again if I spend too much time hanging around before making up my mind. As for when the 'perfect moment' would be, he said he would wait for me. From what he said I sensed that perhaps my parents and I were worrying too much. For even if there is no immediate trigger for the operation, there is some hope; I believe there is a small chance of being able to hear a little bit again, through a brain stem implant. After all, my hearing can't get any worse, can it?

Besides, I want to live without regrets and not with the knowledge that I didn't seize opportunities; although perhaps I will regret this decision, I know that well. Oh, this is so po-intless... But then I wonder: if not now, then when?

I find it so difficult to make the final decision, especially when there are so many uncertainties. Who knows what will happen?

The fact is, I have time now, no school, no studying, no work (my choice). Also, my father is planning to go travelling after his retirement and I don't want him to be away and feel bad about it. Nor do I want to leave it until I am more of a burden than my parents can cope with.

But above all, I just want to be free of the constant worry, the endless deliberating. I want certainty. Even if it turns out to have been the wrong choice, well, so be it. At least I will be free of the goddamned decision and the sword of Damocles hanging over me – especially if it goes well. Whether it will or not, no-one can say, and that is what's holding me back. Why take the risk?

I want my family to support me in my final decision and to respect it. It hasn't been easy. It has taken me seven years to be able to say: now is the right moment – if indeed it is. Maybe I shouldn't think so much but just enjoy life. I try to.

All this is an example of the daily tangle of thoughts that my family and I are trapped in. If we touch on the subject of the operation, someone only has to say, "Why?", and we are stuck again. But even when I'm pissed off when my mother starts yet again with, "why have the operation?", I still love her more than anything. So, for her 60th birthday, I tried to express in poetry what I find so hard to say:

So many things

Where do I begin?
Can't put my feelings into words
just try to let it in
follow the southward swarming birds

Whenever I'm away
you're never far
in this case from the bay
'coz you are my star

Without such strong foundation
I don't think I'd dare
You're the one who built my station
with all your love and care

So many things are only joy
because you paved the way
lining it with tools to employ
for me to walk one day

So many things I find
open-mindedness, honesty, language
strength, humour, being kind
Together they form my courage

For that I'm ever gratified
But with a single flaw
I want you to be satisfied
and celebrate your awe.

Freedom

At the end of 2014 I went travelling again; to San Francisco with my walker. One day I visited the former prison on the island of Alcatraz and found myself wondering what sort of similarities there are between the life of a prisoner and the life of a deaf person? On the tour I stopped by a display board showing an inscription written by a prisoner: "You know there is freedom outside. You can even see it. You dream about it every day. Until one day you are there - and you're terrified. Everything is moving so fast. Everyone is occupied with their tasks. And me? Where do I fit in?" The next group of tourists came along with their audio-guides, all following the instructions on their headphones. I must have looked funny, the only one without headphones, reading from a folder of transcripts. But as I looked at all these people moving from exhibit to exhibit like sheep, I felt different, special, free.

Turning back to the inscription I experienced a rollercoaster of emotions – I was both moved and struck by a sense of yearning. I stood in a trance as the other people moved past me. But for me there was still hope and I clung to that idea as I mingled again with the other tourists. For I, too, will come to the point when I will be faced with the question of how to fit back into society. One day. One day I will be free again. And until then? I am grabbing every bit of freedom for myself that I can get hold of. Or through reading books, just like the prisoners. Or even better by travelling. Of course travelling alone is a bit crazy. What am I doing here? No-one knows me, or my story, or my needs, and so I have to keep starting from the beginning again. "I am deaf. Please write what you are saying." The reactions vary and very few people here, as elsewhere, have any concept of deafness. Some start shouting, others walk away and still others just go on talking so that all I can do is smile and think to myself: "Hello? Who is the deaf one here?" Saying it wouldn't do any good. Maybe I should carry a gong and bang on it?

These people find my situation too challenging. But there are enough people who do actually take the pencil and paper – but then some of them hand it straight back to me. "Oh dear, I think almost amused, but also sighing!" Then I try again: "No. I am deaf and I can't hear what YOU are saying." Finally they begin to write, pass the paper back to me - and what does it say? "It wasn't important." ," Thanks a lot," I say and am none the wiser. Who has the right to decide whether something is important for me? Or interesting? Every time someone opens their mouth they intend to express something that they consider worth mentioning. Why am I denied the right to know what that is? Some of them say "You can talk perfectly well." "Yes," I say, "I learned it when I was a child, like you."

So it takes quite a lot of determination to speak to a stranger at all now because the barrier between us has become so great. More like a fissure between rocks actually, which is slowly growing. Occasionally there are exceptions. People who are prepared to engage with my problems and to take the time, for instance, to show me the way by walking a little way with me or help me in other ways that I could hardly expect. A few will enter the unknown and instinctively start using their hands while they speak slowly. These people offer me openness, kindness and tolerance and I am happy to respond in the same way. They are people who think it is worth making an effort. You can find them everywhere.

Looked at (dis)passionately I suppose I miss about 80% of life's experiences between humans: Language, dialects, accents, nationalities, people talking to me from somewhere I can't see and all the other opportunities to start having a conversation, experiencing new things, hearing sounds from the immediate environment and all the conversations abandoned or those which didn't even take place because of the difficulties in communication. Multiply that by the whole range of information contained in every acoustic experience that I miss and all the other missed opportunities, the list gets longer and longer. On a packed subway train, for instance, where they have no display and the windows are darkened, I have to concentrate hard on counting the stops because I can't hear the announcements. Stupidly I have sat down by the window seat, so I can't see much and I can't risk getting up to look at the map because of my poor balance.

There are a lot of activities that I am not mobile enough to do. I just have to give them a miss. I can't visit Chinatown, for instance, because the streets are too steep. So I go to a café instead and sit in a corner and observe the coming and going. No-one knows me or takes any notice of me.

But I am not lonely. Just alone. The remaining 20% of experiences feel more like 99% to me. Where else could I truly experience unknown things, where else could I fill my dull life with colour and feed my brain with impressions and unforgettable experiences? Where else would I have the chance to meet friendly and helpful people who give me the opportunity to step out of my comfort zone? Without any ties I can simply stop and look at things as I notice them. Round this corner? Into that bar? Browse in that little shop? Let's have a look – why not?

I am always changing my plans, sometimes out of necessity, like Chinatown, sometimes because I have taken on too much, but sometimes simply because I feel like going down this or that little street to look around and see what it's like. It just looks inviting. I am free and can do what I like and no-one will mind. People look at me oddly when they see the walker with a suitcase strapped to it; pushed by a young man who looks drunk. But quite a few offer help if they see that I need it, up a step or over a threshold. They help me over every obstacle. Everything becomes so easy and possible. And if no-one offers help, I just ask. "No problem!" They help, we smile at each other, and they disappear into the crowd.

Last summer I also went to Catalonia on my own. It was great. One day I took a taxi to the famous long beach promenade at Barcelona. I intended to stroll along some of it, with plenty of breaks, to the tram stop from where I could get back to the hostel. But I had been over-ambitious and by about half-way I was exhausted. I was incapable of going any further and took a taxi all the way back to the hostel, where I had to spend the whole of the next day resting. But I wasn't upset that I hadn't achieved my goal, on the contrary, I was just happy to have been there. It means so much to me that the smallest things can make me happy; whether it is ordering a meal in a beach bar in Spanish and finding that the waitress understands me at once or having a refreshing siesta in a park. What a view of that endless beach! And all these interesting people. Marvellous! But three weeks were enough. Three weeks of non-stop new experiences. I even went into the sea - at a beach near the little town of Roses, about 100 km north of Barcelona - thanks to the help of my Couchsurfing host who held me while I floundered in the water with a happy smile on my face. ("Couchsurfing.org" is an international network of private hosts offering a couch or similar as a bed for travellers for free). I thought I could hear the noise of the waves, it was as if the sound had never gone away. Isn't the human brain amazing? I only occasionally spoke English, but my Spanish had been thoroughly put to the test and all the Spaniards said I spoke it well. I went to Gran Canaria to visit Vinay, a fellow student at Southampton, against whom I stood little chance at FIFA (even when he selected 1 star team India and me 5 star FC Barcelona), and there, after exchanging a few words with a waiter, he brought me the menu in Spanish, rather than English or German. That made me happy. I was proud of myself. I had learned the language without being able to hear it.

Future paths

In April of this year I fulfilled a dream of mine – I went to Cuba on a tour with my friend René who is also deafened. It was another unforgettable experience. What a world!

Before setting off I armed myself with four small conversation notebooks for people to write in. They also serve as store of memories. Apart from my sign language conversations with René I spoke nothing but Spanish for 20 days. In the Casa Particular (one of a government managed, but basically privately owned, B&B scheme operating in the country) in Trinidad, where we were staying, we met a family from Germany and exchanged our stories a bit. The last thing they wrote in my notebook was: "You are brave!" I asked: "Do you speak Spanish?" They shook their heads. "You are brave," I said. It's just the different way I am. On the plane René had talked about feeling "the same, but different." I liked that expression so much that I almost used it as the title of this book. On the first day we went on a tour of the old town in a cycle taxi and saw a lot. We were thoroughly shaken around but I would never have managed it on foot with my walker.

Arriving in Havana with our luggage at the blue painted door of our next Casa Particular, we were welcomed by the owner who came down from the first floor to show us up. I was faced with a narrow stone staircase with steep steps. A kind passer-by carried my suitcase and other people helped me up. I hadn't really expected a lift but that was so nice of that man. Putting down his bike and helping carrying the luggage upstairs. Once upstairs we began to plan what we would do the next day. The guidebook suggested a route which wasn't too long but included quite a few interesting things. It could be done in three hours it said. We decided to set aside the whole of the next day to try to do it. And we very nearly succeeded. It took us over potholed streets and broken paving stones to the old town where there seemed to be an endless fiesta going on in every street. So many people ...

With our next Casa particular, out in the country in the tobacco growing area of Viñales where there were more oxen and horses than cars, we hit the jackpot again. Our hosts were extremely kind and took us arouundin a friend's blue Lada - which they started by touching two wires together. And so we came again to a Caribbean beach where I went into the sea, with help, and was spellbound once more by the 'noise' of the waves. Then we went back to Juanito and Maria's brightly painted house and played cards on the veranda and watched the sun disappearing behind the mountains. It didn't matter that the house was on a farm track and the surrounding area virtually inaccessible to me, the place was pulsating with life right in front of me. The Guajiros – tobacco farmers - always had a friendly greeting for us tourists as they returned to the village on their horses or tractors from a hot day's work, while pigs, hens, cats and lizards wandered about the dry garden in front of the house.

Back in Havana we were at a restaurant again where, as so often, a group of musicians were playing. At the end, when they came round collecting money, we announced that we hadn't heard anything. Sorted! It certainly has some advantages, this deafness.

And back at home in Germany, my mother asked, "Aren't

you sad that you can't hear music?" "Of course," I said "but I don't think about it too much. Would I have gone to Cuba only to be sad about what I can't have? "

Instead I am really happy that I can communicate with people in Spanish. OK, I can't hear it, but so what? I can read it, write it and speak it. So that's 3-1 to me!

I came back from Cuba feeling very humbled and more determined to value the things we have in the west because the Cubans have nothing. At least not from our perspective. While I was there I was actually looking forward to what would happen when I got home. I was due to have another operation to remove some skin tumours. It was quite funny to be wearing a hotel 'all-inclusive-guest' wristband in Cuba and one week later to swap it for a hospital identity band.

Even if I was looking forward to this procedure, no operation is fun (except for the anaesthetic, I love that moment when your consciousness fades away) and most are not without risks. I am convinced that a cure for NF2 will be found in five to ten year's time. But even if it isn't, our quality of life is already much better than it was ten years ago thanks to the development in everyday communications – smartphones, internet, etc. – and I expect things will go on improving. Besides, I will have lived in faith, and that's what counts, isn't it? The day will come, I am certain of it. And if it doesn't, well, it doesn't matter. I have never given up hope, but nor have I staked everything on it. Faith is a great support in whatever form it comes. Sometimes I start thinking about what it will be like when I can hear this or that sound again. When I imagine that moment I find myself close to tears and I sit and lose myself in a daydream. What is it like, hearing today? What has been happening since …?

If only NF2 weren't so rare, the research into it would have progressed a lot further by now, because it would be more profitable. As it is, progress is very slow but at least it is moving in the right direction. In the end, this, like most things, is down to money.

I still have my CD collection. At the moment it is not part of my life, but we'll see... For the prospects look good for us, not only thanks to the medical progress in gene therapy, nerve transplantation, and better drugs than Avastin but through technical progress as well, and I am optimistic about the future. The ABI (Auditory Brainstem Implant), which delivers some sounds, is not off the table for me either. And so on, and so on... I am looking forward to the day when everything will be better but at the same time trying to keep my feet on the ground and remain realistic. Because if you live too much in hope you are not living in the present; but in a time that doesn't (yet) exist. Better not to think about it too much. And yet I do still have these moments.... I guess hope dies last.

The year 2015 for me is a year of sport as I work to strengthen my body and relentlessly pursue my goal of walking unaided. Last autumn I bought a tricycle and now that the spring sunshine is here, I ride it along beside the river Main. Benedikt, the son of the Webers who founded the German NF2 self help group almost 25 years ago, is now running it himself together with four other NF2 people, including me. He works tirelessly and is full of fresh ideas and he has become a good friend. Together we work on various projects to benefit NF2ers, exchanging ideas, collecting donations, and, most importantly, organising meetings to try to bring us all out of the isolation that we struggle with every day. Bene initiated the now annual sports event. It started with a marathon and developed into a triathlon to give NF2 people and their friends the opportunity to try out cycling, running and swimming. A couple of years ago I went as a supporter. The cheeky Bene organised somewhere for me to stay, which was great – apart from the FC-Bayern bed linen!

This year I was determined to take part in the triathlon and practised for months, reaching a cycling distance of 14 kilometres. But then the organiser said it would be better for me not to take part because I cycled too 'slowly'. Swallowing my disappointment I still went to the event and as I watched the triathlon I realised that it had been the right decision. So I supported our people from the side-lines again, sitting on my tricycle which I had brought along partly out of defiance but also because I can get around more easily on it than on foot. Goal missed? Well, next time!

I have also started climbing again. While the others spend all day climbing to the top via several different routes, I go my own way. Reaching a height of two metres three times in a day is an enormous experience for me. I guess it is not so different from the feeling the 'normals' get when they reach the top. Or perhaps it is? For added to mine is a burst of pride and gratitude.

When I was practising on my tricycle in Wurzburg I declared war on my weaker self. NB: the 'weaker self' is a translation of the widely known German expression 'pigdog'.

The Pig-Dog

On Sunday morn' at nine
My eyes opened
And how else should it be?
Things followed their course

Slowly it dawned on me
Didn't I want to cycle today?
So out of the cot
A clear-cut plan so far

So I sat up and looked to the side
On my shoulder a little red figure
'Aren't you tired? I mean, we both know:
You only fell asleep at 4. '

I turned my head
And looked at the left shoulder
There sat a little white pixie
And raised her chin so sweet.

He said: 'oh you can sleep afterwards'
What about our plan?
If not now, then when?'
I sank back to bed, no verve

And they argued on and on
I had enough of this clamour
And had to decide.
Result: 5 miles and more

Waiting

Months later. Still the time hasn't come. Not quite. But I have decided, 100% to 0%. The big operation is going to happen. I wasn't in a good state psychologically before the decision and had somehow gotten into a downward spiral until I finally brought the subject up again and wrote to my surgeon, saying: "Right, I am ready." From that moment on I have noticed that the spiral is slowing down. I have found a way to put a stop to it. It wasn't a decision made in desperation because I was now convinced that it was the right thing to do. As each day passes I find that I am more sure that I want this operation; the uncertainty has left me and I am regaining my inner stability. We will see what the outcome will be. I have great hopes and even greater dreams, but, as before, I am trying to keep my expectations low. All I can do now is wait for the date of the operation to come. It is a difficult time and I am once again riding my roller coaster of emotions; some days are bad, others good. I am gradually winding down my activities because it is impossible to know how I will be afterwards. Certainly the operation will mean another big change in my life; the first stage will be just to recover and get myself back on track. Perhaps it will be the start of a new, happier phase of my life? Or perhaps it won't. Now that I have made the decision at least I can stop constantly wondering. Whatever happens will happen. And now I am looking forward to being in hospital again and having it all behind me.

At the moment I am going through the process of waiting, a good time - although it also makes me queasy. But it is teaching me again to cherish the things I have; the people around me who think about me and who make me feel that I am worth something, all the precious time with my family and friends. And what is even more noticeable is that, leaving aside the emotional chaos, I am in better mental health than I have been for a long time. So much so that my family, friends, and especially Annemarie, have managed to distract me from thinking about the operation and make me laugh. One happy event follows another and each one is special. The reunion with Manuel, cooking with Alex, laughing with my sister, a trip to Freiburg to see Sebbo, a lovely weekend with Annemarie at Tempelhof, every moment spent with my parents and much more.

On what was to be my last climbing session at the sports centre before my operation I set a new personal record and achieved my latest goal. I reached the top three times. I kept slipping down again because of the poor co-ordination of my legs but I didn't give up. Never. I just kept fighting on and on. It is a brilliant way to build up strength, co-ordination, balance and, more importantly, the sport is psychologically energising. Problems are solved, possibilities explored and unknown strengths revealed. And it wasn't only good for me; my father came with me every time and stood below to secure the ropes. His pride and happiness were obvious. But after the third climb I had had enough, I knew that my muscles would be aching in the next few days.

As a sort of diary, I now have a 'memory box', a wooden treasure chest which I picked up at a car boot sale. It contains all kinds of mementos; postcards from friends, tickets, letters, photos, diaries, notebooks with messages written during all sorts of encounters that I can no longer remember. Every morning I pick out three of these mementos which bring back memories long buried in my subconscious and I am often moved by how kind friends were, by the things I have done and the places I have been to. Some things no longer seem as important as I thought, others have grown in significance, just as happens in life. Perhaps this time of waiting is an important one after all...

As so often happens in uncertain times like these, new opportunities seem to open up, new possibilities emerge and new dreams are formed and I almost feel that I am floating with shining eyes towards a new vicious circle of happiness. But only almost, for I know that quite soon I shall be far removed from this life. After all, nerves heal extremely slowly.

And of course, now more than ever, my thoughts are on the outcome of the operation, in fact this is the only subject that occupies my mind. I think too, about the end of life, and even though I can't really imagine this happening, I am plagued by doubts about the operation. Have I, in making this decision, decided to end my own life? Currently, I am working on my will. Well, why not? Death is part of life, after all, and this seems a good moment to make mine. However, I don't think it will be needed soon and even if thoughts of death do occur to me, I am fairly certain that things will go well. In a strange way, it is quite fun determining what will become of me and my possessions, and especially planning my funeral. Not exactly a cheerful subject, but strange, comic almost. I am surprised to find that I am currently living quite happily through this time of strain and uncertainty.

Life

Every beginning has an end
And in between is meaning
towards the goal, perhaps some twists and turns
but an end also means a new beginning

As certain as the sunrise,
that's how life begins
continues, starts again
enchants and fascinates us

And our future we create ourselves
Each on his own and all together
we all live in the same world
and the way we are will shape it

And every decision, every choice
happens for a reason
whatever comes
We are allowed to live, day by day

The way of life of each of us
can mean bad things or good
for all, since everything is connected
everything we do returns to us in another way

So let's send out some love
love for the planet and every person
that's how it's strengthened, the cycle of life
for we all know: life is precious

When I was four years old I hadn't yet collected many memories. But I had started acting. My kindergarten must have put on a play. I can't remember much about 'Frederick the Mouse' and yet it must have made an impression on me because the story seems to apply to me now. While all the other mice in the little mouse family are busy working and gathering food Frederick lies at home relaxing, or so it seems. But when the others ask him why he is not doing anything, he answers that he is gathering words, sunbeams and colours. When winter comes and all the food stocks are used up, Frederick tells the other little mice stories about bright meadows, the warm sun and he recites poems. Then all the mice feel warm and comfortable in their mice-brains. I am just like Frederick. I am very lazy. Oh, and I like collecting words as you, reader, will have noticed; although I only write poetry occasionally. For me, playing with everyday words is important. I have come to realise that I am never happier than when I have some wordplay going on in my head. I love twisting each word, each sentence, until it turns into something nonsensical or a pun. And I love making silly words out of a mixture of German and English words. Making my mother laugh at these is a great reward for me.

Annemarie and I spent a wonderful weekend at Tempelhof. After she had left the sun came out and seemed to smile on me all day long; I gathered the sunbeams. In the evening I asked Pascal's partner, Inna, what she thought of Annemarie. She answered with one word: "Sunny." I don't often find myself speechless – but this was the perfect description.

Finally the day came. I packed my bag once more and set off for the hospital. In the entrance there is a large model stork where they write the names of all the babies born that day –

"Today's Arrivals." In the list we spotted, "Frederik", spelled just like my name. I smiled as I continued to the ward and saw the nurse's familiar faces.

It was beautiful in the hospital's city, Erfurt. My father was with me, we went to an Italian or a Chinese restaurant or a good plain German one between Erfurt and Weimar. It goes without saying that the restaurant was called, "The Sun", and indeed the sun shone down on us every day. On the last day before the operation we went to Erfurt Garden Park, a large ornamental park, and we thought at first there would not be much to see as it was now autumn. Far from it! We were greeted by thousands of dahlias of every possible colour. The trees everywhere were in their radiant autumn colours of green, yellow and red, and I marvelled again and again at how many different shades of colour were on show. The car journey from my home to the hospital with coloured treens lining the motorway had already been an absolute spectacle. So here they were: the colours! Everything was packed and ready and now I felt I could face the ordeal to come. I didn't feel nervous while I was waiting. I was cheerful; with occasional brief moments of anxiety which quickly went away again. They were unimportant. On the day before my operation I sat in my wheelchair again and normal life began to fade away. I felt as if I was on a mission and that I wasn't really part of normal life anymore. I had begun to feel this strongly when visiting Erfurt's 'Oktoberfest', a small fun fair with a beer tent. But no matter. I was happy now that the waiting seemed to be over. I was doing everything I could to be in good shape and my father was proud of all the hygienic measures I was taking, which is not normal for me. And yet the scan taken on the day I arrived at the hospital showed signs of a persistent sinus infection I'd had. Traces of it were still there. On top of that, my surgeon was not feeling entirely well himself. So on the evening before the operation we were told: postpone the operation by a week, but stay on the ward. "OK. I can cope with one more week", I thought. Of course I was briefly disappointed, but only briefly, because I quickly realised that it was a sensible decision, the infection was not getting any better – why take the risk? Both parties need to be 100% well. At the end of the week I still needed more antibiotics, so the operation was postponed again and a new date was fixed for two months later. Somehow I didn't mind too much. So now what? Well, I could visit friends, perhaps travel a bit, though probably not much, publish my book – but above all, just wait. The waiting gnaws at me and saps my energy, so it is vital to find plenty of activity in order not to sink into a dark hole. I have already made a list of activities and I have some more ideas for travel. And in December 2015, the operation.

And after that, when I have recovered, what will I do then? I have no idea. Go to Mexico, perhaps? I am suddenly reminded of the beach at Roses in Catalonia and my stay there last summer. It seems that even there it is sometimes cloudy, and occasionally it rains, and one morning my host looked out and said gloomily, "Today is not a beautiful day." "

That's alright," I said, "My day is beautiful every day."
He smiled.

Change of perspective

On the next few pages, my family writes a few words about their perspective.

Mummy

September 2003. When Frederik and I were suddenly standing at the entrance to the neurosurgery department for our first appointment, I thought to myself, this can't be happening. It was horrifying. My stomach was in knots and my heart was racing. We were entering a completely new world. When I discovered later on what kind of dramas were taking place in people's lives at the hospital, I wanted nothing more than to wave a magic wand and leave this place far behind as fast as possible. But here we were. This had become our reality.

But what I didn't know at the time was that the remnants of our shattered lives would be stitched back together in the years to come while Frederik's hearing loss became worse and ultimately led to complete deafness. It still makes me sad just imagining that he cannot hear the birds singing and the sound of water flowing. And the music! It causes me so much heartache that it is hard for me to enjoy these things without shedding a tear or two.

I searched for a plausible reason for every small change we noticed, like when he texted me from his new school in Munich saying, 'Mummy, my voice is going crazy.' My response was something along the lines of, 'Well, you didn't wear your anorak and it was freezing at the train stop. Where was your scarf?' It was hard to not get nervous, especially when we started to notice even bigger changes later on, and not just physical ones.

Nowadays I don't wish that things could be like they were before. Instead I am learning to relish the moment. This is a lesson that all of us have probably learned over the past few years.

But things have got better and today we are trying to cope with the practical challenges in daily life, like the lack of accessibility in many public areas for physically disabled people.

In Wurzburg there aren't any lifts at the train station, as the city decided to spend money on renovating the fountain instead. Moreover, there aren't any train employees who feel obliged to help disabled travellers with their luggage or wheelchair get from the train station tunnel to the platforms above. Instead, I remember when they just stood there and stared. I could easily come up with a long list of such examples, especially when it comes to German train stations.

Then there is the fact that subtitles are rarely used for films in the cinema or are seldom available on the telly, even in the ENT Hospital no less! Discrimination is everywhere. And then there is the degradation and humiliation that people with special needs feel as a result of encounters with administrators who are not sensitised to their needs or other people who do not know how to deal with people who have disabilities. I remember the time that the butcher nonchalantly wanted to offer teenage Frederik a piece of sausage, like he normally does for little children. Thank God I intervened and prevented Frederik from becoming aware of it. If he had noticed, he would have wanted to disappear from sight, or would have blushed out of embarrassment, or would have become furious.

A similar thing happened with a lolly in a restaurant. As a mother, I felt so humiliated! Not to mention the ongoing battles with the insurance company. All these little things make life really hard, and I feel powerless and sad at the same time. So you could say that we have been going through a lot of new experiences, but they are making us stronger and stronger. Our family has grown closer. We are fighting together.

We have also noticed that new doors have opened up for Frederik and us, too – through you, Anne Bouwmeester; through you, Erika Bogar; through you, Nicola; and through you, dear Brigitte. We keep marching on driven by the new strength we've gained along the way and are especially motivated by Frederik's incredibly strong willpower and fighting spirit.

We tried to learn sign language, but it isn't easy. I am still not able to use sign language for every single uttered word and I have to concentrate really hard to understand what is being said because German is also not my mother tongue and people tend to speak so quickly, they mumble or there is too much background noise. And there you have it: I discriminate against him myself, too! Much too often! It's a terrible feeling. It would only be fair not to exclude him, but I find it very time consuming and nerve-racking. I imagine that for him it must seem like the feeling you have when you are surrounded by a group of Japanese and can't understand much of what is being said or maybe nothing at all. You just sit there and can't join in on the conversation. But the learning process continues for all of us.

Over the years I have learned to accept that everyone has a cross to bear. It's part of life. Frederik never showed any bitterness or asked, 'Why me?' He just goes humbly through life. I am proud that he has been able to network with many people and that he is building bridges by volunteering to teach sign language courses or by working for the self-help group. He has also helped set up a group in England for bringing people with NF2 together. He acts as a disseminator of information, a networker.

Frederik can be quite stubborn and is very determined, which is probably the reason why he has achieved so much. Not many people would dare to travel to Cuba carrying a suitcase on a walker.

Life with Frederik is quite adventurous. Apart from the walker, the new tricycle he bought has been the best investment thus far. Last week he had to struggle up the old back staircase at his doctor's office because the building is not wheelchair accessible (you would think a general practioner's office would be wheelchair accessible). The two healthy, but bored teenagers who were sitting on the stairs commented on his bike: 'Wow, cool bike, man'. Of course, he didn't hear what they said, but I did, and I could proudly tell him what they said in sign language with a smile on my face. Even those two kids got a taste of Frederik's positive approach to life.

There's a story I would like to share with you which captures just the kind of person he is. When he was in his first year of school he went to a school psychologist, who told me later, 'You know, your son is very special. We really have two Frederiks to deal with'. My response was, 'Well, he is after all a Gemini.' He was born in June on a bank holiday, although it isn't a holiday anymore. Everything comes in twos with him: two parents, two siblings, later on - two nieces, by now - two walkers and tricyles, and even two tumours. This year was his first year gardening and he also harvested two aubergines and two peppers, and even his disease is called 'type 2'. Moreover, the title of one of his papers for university was even 'Between Two Worlds' – the hearing and not hearing. He's had one foot

in England and one in Germany. And then there is his great
love: words. He knows them all in English and German and
has fun playing with their double meanings!

Frederik has little difficulty making decisions. He knows
exactly what he wants. As a family we have learned together
with him that life has many open doors – not only two. And
it is exciting. As we often say, that's 'Frederik life': exciting.

A topic that's come up again and again is my continual and
increasing fear. My family often brings it up. I don't know
whether it is connected with Frederik's disease or not, but my
fears often stem from my thoughts of impending catastrophe,
which makes it hard for me to sleep well at night. Sometimes
I wish I could go to a life-coach who could help me deal with
my fantasies better. Someone like the German TV personality
and psychologist Ms Kallwass would be great.

The worst period for me was after Frederik's second operation when he was really fighting for his life.

During his stay in the hospital, he couldn't speak, eat or hear.
I think I am probably still affected by that traumatic experience, even today. In some situations, like when he swallows the
wrong way or has coughing fits, I start recalling these images
and my fear comes back again.

Another point that bothers me is that I think I expect too
much from my children. I think as a result of my insecurities,
which are usually related to Frederik, I start to annoy them
and drive them away from me. I don't know how to deal with
such an extreme situation, and for me, it is still an extreme
situation. I am confronted with my child's disease on a daily
basis – and it's been over ten years. My GP and other parents

in the same situation have repeatedly recommended that I go on to a rehabilitation centre/wellness spa for psychological support. Maybe it is something worth trying. Who knows.....

But what me really made sad is that I had the feeling he had missed out on enjoying a few important years in his life: the rites of passage in puberty and having fun spending time with friends without a care in the world. Basically doing all the things that teenagers do.

But the thing that has really helped me during the dark times has been my incredible girlfriends; they have cheered me up and given me the strength to carry on. Being able to share my suffering, sorrow and fears has helped me so much and still helps me to this day.

I am learning how to deal with the images in my head and to live more in the moment. Its is quite a challenge!

And Frederik, remember I am so proud of you and love you to the bottom of my heart!

Daddy

My perspective as a father during Frederik's journey with the neurofibromatosis type 2 disease, which began in September 2003.

When I look back at our summer holidays in Cornwall in August 2003, I realise that was the point in time when we began to notice that Frederik's hearing was beginning to get worse. There was something not quite right with the way he was walking, in a swerving line to the toilet facilities at the camping site. At first, I thought it might have something to do with adolesence and that he was just tuning out what his parents were saying. I even thought that maybe he had discovered alcohol. But once we got back home to Wurzburg, we went to an ENT specialist who was supposed to remove the lumps of earwax in his ears. My assumption that his problems were nothing serious couldn't have been more wrong. By the end of all the tests and examinations he had been diagnosed with neurofibromatosis type 2.

Initially, I did not realise the full impact that this insidious disease could have. I thought when a person goes to hospital, they have a procedure done and they leave hospital all healthy again. But with NF2 that is sadly not the case. I needed a year to realise what this disease meant for our family and to come to terms with our new situation. I withdrew from my social circles. I just couldn't stand hearing other people's stories which were meant to calm me down or were intended to get me to relate to a story about someone else's medical history that friends and acquaintances wanted to share. I didn't want to hear about any of what I considered to be trivial problems that other people had. I also judged our 'friends', who distanced themselves from us and I considered their distance as a personal insult. It was only a few years later that I understood that these people simply didn't know how to deal with serious illnesses and that it had nothing to do with me or us personally. After the first operation for the acoustic neuroma in his left ear, the doctors recommended that Frederik undergo rehabilitation treatment at a special centre near the Lake of Constance in Southern Germany.

During his stay in the rehabilitation centre Frederik became completely deaf; the only way we could communicate with him was by writing messages back and forth to each other. We also had to admit that rehab wasn't helping him recover and his stay there was more of a psychological strain on him than anything else; he had been suddenly thrown into an environment with severely mentally and physically disabled people where he really didn't belong. After my attempts to take suitable steps from a distance proved to be in vain, we decided to basically 'kidnap' him from the rehabilitation centre and bring him home where he could receive further treatment from the ENT hospital in our area. During the 'kidnapping', my wife kept a lookout at the nurses' station while Frederik and I packed his things and brought them to the car.

A big turning point over the years of living with the disease was in 2008, when he had the second major operation for his acoustic neuroma in his left ear. After this operation he began a nearly six-month struggle, which started in at the intensive care unit, continued in the semi-intensive care ward and ended with caring for him ourselves at home. His condition improved extremely slowly and there were some periods where it hardly improved at all. That is when I began to learn how to use sign language, which I found really difficult to learn. That is also when I began to understand that there was an important difference between people who were deaf from birth and those who became deaf during their lives due to accidents or illnesses, like in Frederik's case. I took courses at the local adult educational centre and even got special permission to take a course in German sign language at a university. Upon starting the course, I had to accept the fact that learning at my age (50) was not as easy as it was for the 20 year old students in the class. The really hard thing about German sign language (DGS) is that it has its own grammar, sentence structure and writing system which contains references to gestures and facial expressions.

In fact, DGS is not really the right method of communication for our situation with Frederik since it is not based on German and he grew up speaking and hearing German until he was 17. Just to give you an idea of how different they are, here is an example of a sentence in Signed German (LBG) and DGS: in Signed German we say the equivalent to 'Please give me the glass' and in DGS 'Glass give' (with the corresponding gesture that I want the glass and don't want to give a glass, as well as additional facial expression indicating the 'please' element to the sentence). Frederik would not expect me to suddenly start speaking to him in this way. Given our situation, this is why we only use Signed German (LBG) together with the hand signs and movements from German Sign Language (DGS). This way we can keep the German grammar and sentence structure. I admit that I still struggle with remembering all the different signs I have learned and I forgot many of them when Frederik spent four years in England studying. So it is no surprise that there are often misunderstandings and sometimes it ends up causing anger and frustration on both our parts.

But let's go back to the rehabilitation period after the second big operation. The convalescence period after his interrupted four month rehabilitation period was a real challenge for our family because we had to provide nursing care without having much knowledge on how to do it and without much support from doctors, associations and organisations. Frederik required a high level of nursing care. It wasn't rare for alarms from pumps or other machines to wake us up at night and some of the machines, like the feeding tube, ran day and night. If the tube got bent or Frederik swallowed the wrong way again, the suction catheter had to be pushed through the trachea into the lungs so that the nutrients meant for the stomach could be removed from the lungs. This was very important for preventing pneumonia from developing.

These types of emergencies usually happened when the nurse who provided home nursing care for 30 minutes a day was not around. After three months, we gave up the idea of being able to handle the nursing care ourselves when we had found out by coincidence that we had the right to receive intensive nursing care services at home. During this period of his illness, I reduced my working hours at the university of applied sciences where I was working to 70% and I accepted a cut in my salary. Later on I was able to set up an office at home, which was such a godsend. I was so lucky to have an employer that had so much understanding for my situation and was willing to accommodate my needs. Without their help I wouldn't have been able to deal with the challenges we were facing.

We were also increasingly becoming aware of the fact that the set-up of our cosy house was not suitable for taking care of a family member in need of nursing care; the house had narrow stairs, doorways that were too narrow for a wheelchair, and other barriers like doorsills leading to the rooms or the terrace. Even the two steps to the garden were enough to prevent Frederik from being able to move around independently and go outside by himself. When he wanted to get some fresh air, it required a lot of assistance. We decided to buy a flat in the city which could be built to meet the needs of disabled and elderly individuals, since the block of flats were still being constructed. Now we have the peace of mind that we can turn a room into an intensive care unit or nursing ward whenever we need to, which is so important because this disease is so unpredictable.

I often had to act as a mediator between Frederik and the nurses, who worked in shifts and lived with us 20 hours a day.

Sometimes they weren't meeting his needs and sometimes the chemistry just wasn't there. I remember how one nurse who also had a son the same age as Frederik would get teary-eyed whenever she would see Frederik lying there helpless. Frederik would act snippy and made it very clear that he didn't want her sympathy but just her help. There were many wonderful moments with the nurses, too, during the two and half years when he needing nursing care. Having their support helped me a lot because they had a lot more experience than I did with these types of situations.

A miracle happened in the spring of 2010 after Fredrik underwent anti-body therapy. One day Frederik stood up out of his wheelchair without any help and started to do things by himself. He began once again to live an independent life.

I won't go into detail about the fights we had along the way with the health insurance company and government aid organisations as well as with the state-run health insurance for civil servants because they would fill up a book. But I do have one story, which is worth mentioning, namely the time when an electric wheelchair was finally approved for Frederik. The decisive factor for the authorities was not the fact that Frederik would be able to move around without assistance, but instead I had to prove that the people assisting him would not be able to push him around in a normal wheelchair to go to places like physical therapy, since the ramp leading into the practice was very steep. On the other hand I don't want to be unfairly critical of our health insurance companies; if we had been living in the USA our family would have presumably gone broke a long time ago.

The years while Frederik was away at university in England were admittedly more relaxed. He had this opportunity thanks to the university's approach to real inclusion of disabled young adults at their institution and the generous financial support of the British government and university, regardless of his parents' financial status. While he was in England our life almost got back to 'normal'. However, there were a few critical situations, but we had acquired some good routines by then.

A very emotional moment for me was at Frederik's graduation when he received his Bachelor's degree in Modern Languages. He received a very long round of applause by the whole auditorium for his above-average achievements. I was so incredibly proud of my son, who achieved so much due to his diligence and stubbornness, a trait which I often hate because it makes my life more difficult at times.

I know the dark cloud that has loomed over us all these years will not completely disappear from sight. Sometimes it hovers directly above us and sometimes it is far off in the distance. But whenever it's directly over us, we know how to mobilise ourselves in order to give Frederik the support he needs. And when there is no dark cloud overhead…we have learned to relax and regain our strength so that we are ready for the next storm.

Casi (sister)

I can still remember how one day I was sitting around and thinking about my life. At the time, everything seemed to be running smoothly and there were no big or even small crises happening in my personal life, like what some of my friends were going through. Their parents were getting divorced or they couldn't find an apprentice position. Then I thought about whether life was maybe preparing me for something bad to happen and that it had spared me up until then in order to make me strong. Well, the honeymoon could only last for so long.

After I finished my training as an occupational therapist, I got a job and drove to an advanced training course in Recklinghausen. When I was there I got a call from my parents who were crying on the phone. They told me the shocking news that Frederik had more than 30 tumours in his body and he had to have emergency surgery. It was so surreal because of all the coincidences:

– I was in Recklinghausen, which is also one of the names of the disease

– The advanced training course I was taking was about the brain, nerves and everything to do with hearing.

– The thoughts I described above were coming true: Life had been preparing me for being able to handle a major twist of fate. And here it was in full force!

Once I returned home our focus was on trying to process and deal with everything that was happening and to learn to accept the situation. I know a lot about this process from my consultation meetings with patients at work. The only thing is that the distance that a person can have at work suddenly disappears when it is happening to someone in their family.

I found Frederik's situation really hard to deal with. At work I didn't let the pain affect me but the tears started flowing as soon as I was alone in my car driving home. I even ended up having a car crash once.

Looking back, I can remember some positive and negative things about this period in our lives. My first visit to his hospital bed after the surgery was horrible; I felt so helpless just seeing him lying there with so many tubes and wires attached to his body and I slowly realised what an impact this awful disease could have on Frederik's life.

He was lying in bed and counted the rings on the curtain that separated his bed from the others in the intensive care unit. He talked about the strange things that he perceived during the operation, like huge machines which were moving some kind of discs around and basketball players who were flying through the air.

Then Frederik completely lost his hearing and the rehabilitation centre where he was staying turned out to be the completely wrong place for him. No one knew anything about deafness there and it was more of a hospital for teenagers who liked going to the cinema or the disco. He couldn't take part in any of the social activities and could only communicate by writing notes. I felt so sorry for him!

One can't help but ask, 'Why him?' or 'What did he do to deserve this?' I was the kind of person who believed that justice in life is somehow balanced, but now it seemed as though there was no justice in the universe.

But there were also really funny situations, too. I can remember how he visited me with our parents in the camper. My mum was, of course, very worried about her son, who wasn't going to pass up a chance to shock her. My mom and I were standing in the garden and the camper was a little off to the side, and then the door opened suddenly. Frederik watched us as we looked at him worried and then he let himself fall out of the door onto the grass. We ran over to him and then he started laughing at us while lying on the grass.

I also recall how he went to a fancy-dress party for carnival after he was released from the hospital. He strapped on some Mickey Mouse ears to his head, stuck a button pin on each ear that had a crossed out ear on it, and then set off for the party. I really admire Frederik for his sense of humour!

Somehow life continued. I moved after getting a new job in the town Rothenburg ob der Tauber and got a little distance from everything going on. But we were always in regular contact with each other. Frederik visited us and we visited him. It has taken time to learn to accept everything that has happened with his health. But he is dealing it rather well because he is such a fighter and we have always stuck together as a family.

Then came the next operation and at the time my daughter was about six months old. When I was pregnant, we knew about the impending operation and Frederik once made the comment that a new soul comes into this world and another one leaves. I was really scared!

The recovery period after this operation was terribly hard; seeing my little brother like that and all the problems that developed. I always tried to be strong when I was with him but the moment I left the room I would break down. He was transferred to Neustadt for rehabilitation and we, his family, tried to alternate our visits. It was really hard for me because I had a baby to take care of. Nonetheless we tried to show him our love, to be there for him and to distract him with different things, like taking walks and playing games, etc.

It was not easy once he got back home either. It was hard to see how exhausted my parents were and how much effort they put into his recovery.

It wasn't easy to see my normally strong father weak and crying; my mother was losing more and more weight.

I noticed that I couldn't work in my field anymore. I was annoyed when people were complaining about their 'little problems'. I thought to myself, 'Leave me alone, my brother is fighting for his life and you are complaining that your kid is holding his pen too tightly!' I noticed that other people's problems were making me a little mentally aggressive. It was all just too much and I didn't have the emotional distance that was necessary anymore! My patients with neurological problems reminded me too much of Frederik. Luckily, my boss at the time understood my situation and I could continue to work at the practice but in another area.

How horrible it must have been for Frederik with all the problems that he had: the feeding tube, the trachea cannula, the hearing loss, the physical weakness – all while still being totally mentally fit. And yet he still kept his sense of humour despite it all. Every time he got knocked down by life, he always got back up again, no matter how many times he was knocked down.

I have since learned to accept Frederik's disease, which is something I attribute mostly to him and his way of dealing with things. But sometimes it is still hard to be powerless and helpless. Now that I have my own family and am busy with my daily routine, I often wonder if I am there enough for him.

As far as the future is concerned, I try not to think about it too much. I recently wondered about why I am somewhat unemotional, especially just before his next operation. I admit that sometimes thoughts pop into my mind like, 'Oh God, what will happen if he dies?' But I usually just push these negative thoughts out of my head. I think I am like this because we have become used to dealing with these emotions and it is also a way to protect ourselves.

What is more, life has taught me that life just happens and it usually turns out very differently than you had planned! This is why I am not going to worry about things ahead of time which may not even happen. You could say my image of justice being balanced is basically still tottering back and forth!

To conclude, I can say that we have been down a rocky road together but Frederik alone has proven his strength time and time again. I have a lot of respect for his way of dealing with everything and naturally I hope that we will be in each other's lives for many years to come.

I love you, Fetzi!

Passi

I am Pascal, Frederik's brother, and am 35 years old today (2015).

It is not easy for me to write these lines. Not because I will get emotional or I don't want to think about everything that has happened, but because one of the things that I have learned from years of dealing with Frederik's disease is that life takes place right now. And now. And now..... Nevertheless I want to go back to the beginning, to my first memories, or rather the first time I had an inkling that something wasn't quite right. My words below are basically a summary of my thoughts and feelings which seem important in hindsight. They aren't necessarily in chronological order and don't have any fixed point in time. They are the summation of everything that's happened or what has stayed with me over the years after this rollercoaster ride we have been on.

I remember once we both went rollerblading at the sports ground with a friend of Fetz's. It must have been around 2002. Frederik was 16 and I was 22. I criticised him for being so wobbly on the blades and for not looking up to scratch when he went over the ramp. In retrospect I feel really badly about it. I was really disappointed, because at the time, I was a roller-blade whizz. Afterwards everything happened really fast and when I look back, I think that I was really taken by surprise and overwhelmed by Frederik's situation given the fact that I am the kind of guy who is rather slow at processing emotional issues. For this reason, my strategy was to put myself in an emotionally neutral position and to deal with what is.

It was only years later when I really admitted the pain I was feeling; working through my emotions has helped me deal with the grief and shock of our fate.

Man, was I upset about how unfair life was. Why did something like this happen to my brother? Why him? I was angry and sometimes I was close to hitting someone when I noticed people were making fun of him or weren't being cooperative with him; usually this was because they didn't know about his situation and often there was no bad intention on their part but it still made me so angry! Sometimes I would have liked to let out all of my frustration by hitting one of the mean healthy people out there, who didn't have a care in the world, right in the face.

And then there were often periods of grief. I felt deep sadness about the apparent constraints and restraints in his life after the operations. I mean, just try and imagine me going into hospital as a seemingly healthy teenager and then you wake up and you can't hear anymore! Your balance is gone! Your motor skills in your fingers and hands diminish. At the beginning you can only survive because people feed you, bring you to the toilet, give you oxygen and pump mucous out of your throat or lungs! Your survival depends on being hooked up to so many cool beeping machines.

How should a person deal with this? How should relatives handle this? I have tried to imagine how I would have dealt with being in his situation. Usually I came to the conclusion that I wouldn't have managed it. I would have probably ended up wallowing in misery, depressed and weary of life. But in reality I 'only' have the role of being Frederik's brother. It's my parents who are the ones that have to bear seeing their child like that and are the ones who have to find a way of coping with the situation so that they don't fall apart emotionally. I admire my mum and dad for the way they quickly dealt with situations which were constantly changing and sometimes quite dramaticly, for the way they put their own needs last, and for some of the sacrifices they made.

But back to Frederik:

Frederik's motto seems to be 'just accept things the way they are' and he uses this as the starting point.

Over the past 10 years, I have rarely seen him really sad or in total despair. He has accepted things incredibly quickly and has tried to make the best out of the situation. What is more, he has kept his sense of humour and still has a zest for life.

You wouldn't believe what Frederik did once he started getting better and was out of the wheelchair. He decided to go to university in England and to travel. He set up and joined societies there and made a circle of friends. He even drove around with his car and got to meet women. Over the years, I often thought that the poor guy might die without ever having been intimate with a woman. These dramatic inner thoughts of mine were nothing but rubbish! Completely crazy. The one thing I have come to realise is that of the two of us, I am the one who is more 'disabled'.

People who cut themselves off from the endless opportunities out there in life due to their ideas, views and rigid expectations end up sacrificing one opportunity after the other to have an adventurous, colourful and full life. Frederik is living proof and a constant reminder for me that almost all of the obstacles in one's life are not physical or material but rather in the mind.

My dearest brother, Frederik, thank you for everything, and I mean everything. Thank you for having made this your mission in life and for continuing to make it your mission. You are a real hero who holds his head up high and rises to new challenges day after day.

Excerpt from a letter to my brother in March 2015:
Dear Fetz,

I am writing these lines partly for me as a way of sorting out my thoughts and so that they become easier to grasp. They give me a chance to look at what we've been through more closely and for me to remember how I felt. They will also give you and the rest of the family a chance to understand me better. Maybe you and everyone else will discover similarities and will feel a connection. Ideally they will help us communicate better with each other without fear and will help us so that we can spend time with each other in a more relaxed and less emotionally charged atmosphere. After spending time with you this past week, I have been having the same types of thoughts and feelings like I often used to have when we were together in the past. As usual, I am so proud of you and I have a great deal of respect for your way of life. And as always, I am also deeply concerned about you and I am sad.

My sadness is often combined with anger and I sometimes have to ask myself questions like, 'Have I done enough for you? Have I made enough effort to learn sign language so that I can communicate with you fluently and effortlessly? Have I taken you up on enough of your offers to spend time together, like going with you on holiday? Have I maybe left you alone too often or have I not really concerned myself enough with your feelings and your way of thinking? Have I really done my whole part?' It's not as if I was always sure about what exactly my part in all of this has been! And where does my inner reluctance to fully get involved come from?

One of the main reasons is surely my fear of grief and losing you. Images or thoughts about horror scenarios come to me again and again, like an operation not going well, or that you have an accident while travelling – and I am not there. I realise how hard it is for me to deal with illness and death. Sometimes I just can't bear it.

And you, Fetz, are confronted with it all the time. In a way this whole thing has been a blessing for me because I have learned to appreciate life, my health and the endless opportunities I have. Plus, it makes me realise how unimportant superficial problems are. But at the same time, it's also been a curse because I can only handle being confronted with my 'disability' in certain situations and sometimes I can't come to grips with it at all. When I say my 'disability', I am referring to the unanswered questions I mentioned above and also the question about whether I am really living my life to the fullest. After all, you are the one who is an expert at doing exactly this. In this aspect, you are my teacher. Lastly, as I was writing these lines, I also asked myself, 'What do I want from you?' Absolution? No, of course not, even if the thought of it is somewhat tempting. Right after we talked about the option of undergoing surgery in autumn, I had the feeling that I was able to have more insight into your thoughts and feelings. I understood what an almost inhumane and difficult decision you have to face.

I want to help you with your decision making process. In other words, to help you along your way to making the final decision, because it is you, and you alone, who will have to make it. Let me know whatever it is that I can do to help you make it, and I will see if I am able and willing to give you support.

With love,

Pascal

Appendix: about NF2

Neurofibromatosis type 2 (NF2) is a rare genetic disease that causes tumours to develop throughout the entire central and peripheral nervous system. People who suffer from this disease are confronted with a wide variety of problems.

NF2 affects about one in 35,000 people, regardless of gender or race. Since NF2 is a genetic disorder there is no real 'onset' of the disease; it should be seen as something you are born with. NF2 is primarily a tumour causing disease. The number of tumours and their severity varies from case to case.

The progression of NF2 varies greatly from one patient to the other. Most people with NF2 develop their first symptoms during puberty or in their teens; a few people develop symptoms during childhood but some people do not have any problems at all until they are 40 or 50 years old. The progression of the disease can be very different in each individual; even when those afflicted by the disease come from the same family.

The first symptoms of NF2 often include partial or complete hearing loss, ringing and pinging sounds in the ears (tinnitus) or problems with balance. These symptoms are often accompanied by persistent headaches and dizziness. Sometimes small skin tumours (schwannomas and very rarely neurofibromas) are the first sign of the disease. It is rare for neurological deficits caused by tumours on the spinal column to be the first symptoms of NF2. Many people have vague symptoms for many years before the underlying disease is diagnosed. Since most of the benign tumours caused by NF2 develop rather slowly, it is very likely that they have been growing for many years before the first symptoms are noticed.

Schwannomas and other types of tumours

The most common tumours in NF2 patients are tumours that develop along the auditory nerves, which are known as vestibular schwannomas or acoustic neuromas. These tumours develop along both auditory nerves in almost everyone who has been diagnosed with NF2. The auditory nerves comprise the acoustic (auditory) nerve, which transfers information about sounds to the brain, and the vestibular nerve, which sends information about equilibrium (balance) to the brain.

People with NF2 can also develop tumours on other nerves; the most frequently affected areas are cranial nerves, the spinal column and the peripheral nerves which are located outside the spinal column and brain.

When Schwannomas appear on the cranial nerves, they can result in the loss of nerve function in the area of the neck or head. When they grow larger and put pressure on the brainstem, they can lead to neurological deficits affecting different parts of the body. Schwannomas that grow on the peripheral nerves can cause sensory disturbances, or in rare cases, paralysis in a specific part of the body.

Some tumours can even grow even so big that they put pressure on the spinal cord and cause paresthesias (abnormal sensations), which lead to weakness in the legs. Tumours that grow in nerve bundles in areas like in the armpits or groin can lead to weakness or paralysis in an arm or leg.

Schwannomas can also grow visibly on very small nerves in or on the skin. These schwannomas rarely cause neurological symptoms but they can be painful. They are sensitive to pressure and externally visible. Tumours can also grow inside the nerves and can lead to a progressive loss of function. These tumour formations lead to impairment of nerve conduction and ultimately muscle function; this type of nerve damage is called polyneuropathy.

In addition to the schwannomas, people with NF2 can also develop other types of tumours. Tumours can develop from the membranes that surround the brain and spinal cord. These tumours, which are known as meningiomas, can cause several different neurological symptoms depending on their location. Like with schwannomas, a doctor can discover signs of a tumour being present during a neurological examination, even before the patient notices any symptoms himself. Here it is worth noting that people with NF2 have to monitor themselves very closely since changes tend to develop very slowly, they are often not noticed by the patient, or the patient unwittingly develops methods to compensate for these changes.

Other and concurrent symptoms

One symptom that often accompanies NF2 is the development of malformations in the area of the eyes or other eye abnormalities; these can be diagnosed and should be monitored by an ophthalmologist. Most people with NF2 develop cataracts, which can impair a person's ability to see. It is important for all people with NF2 to have their eyes thoroughly examined by a specialist who is familiar with NF2 so that the right point in time for a surgical intervention can be determined.

Another frequently concurrent symptom of NF2 is functional impairment of facial nerves (nervus facialis). It is typically caused by the previously described schwannomas that grow on the auditory nerve or by their surgical removal, or it can be caused by a tumour developing on the facial nerve itself. It is not rare for tumours that typically affect the vestibular nerves to grow in the area around the facial nerves.

Paralysis of the facial nerve (facial paralysis) can lead to incomplete closure of the eyelids and to dry eyes. Facial paralysis can cause problems with eating, drinking and speaking.

Treatment options for NF2-associated tumours

While in the past the only real treatment for advanced tumours was surgery, now there are other new treatment options available, like radiation and drug therapy. Discussing the options with an experienced NF2 specialist is necessary for deciding which individual method of treatment is best for the given situation.

Treatment option: surgery

Today, the surgical removal of tumours is still the preferred method for treating NF2 tumours in most cases. But there are risks associated with surgery because the tumours tend to lie near the brain and spinal cord. Operations in these small and sensitive areas can cause further damage to the nerves and can lead to new neurological problems. For this reason, an operation should be delayed as long as possible until the point is reached where the risk of further damage by the tumour outweighs the risks posed by having surgery or the person with NF2 can't tolerate the symptoms caused by the tumour any longer.

Treatment option: radiation therapy

Radiation therapy is another method available for treating patients with NF2. It is recommended for patients who cannot have surgery or for patients would suffer additional serious neurological damage if they were to have the tumour surgically removed. There are different medical opinions about the extent to which radiation makes operating conditions more difficult after a patient undergoes radiation. Moreover, the published medical records of NF2 patients indicate that some patients develop a malignant nerve sheath tumour after receiving radiation for an acoustic neuroma.

Treatment option: medication

A new turning point for the treatment of NF2 has been the development of new drugs that target the Schwann cells in a cell culture.

Several different drugs are currently being tested for their efficacy, but it will take several years for researchers to make a conclusion about how effective they are in treating NF2. The medication Avastin (bevacizumab) is generally tolerated well, but it has a number of side-effects that have to be carefully explained to the patient and there is still no information about the long-term effects of taking the drug. Bevacizumab has been used to treat NF2 patients for about seven years.

The experience using the drug up until now has shown that this medication can lead to high blood pressure or vascular damage in the kidneys. For this reason, it is important to check the patient's urine for protein on a regular basis.

The drug's other side-effects include fatigue on the day the drug is administered, an increased susceptibility to illness and missed menstrual periods in women. Lastly, Avastin can also negatively affect men's sperm count and their reproductive system.

Testing methods

When NF2 is diagnosed in a patient, there are a number of tests that can be done to determine the severity of the person's disease and to monitor its progression. The best, or most accurate, methods currently being used are CAT or MRI (magnetic resonance imaging) scans.

An MRI image is used to visualise the anatomy of the body spatially. While an MRI scan is used most often for taking images of the brain, it can also be used for taking images of the spinal cord or the nerves in the arm or legs. Basically, an MRI is a round chamber that is surrounded by magnets. When undergoing an MRI, the patient lies on a gurney, which is slid into the chamber. During the scan, the magnets rotate around the chamber and make a loud banging sound. A contrast agent can be injected into the patient at a special point in time during the scan, so that certain parts of the brain or body can be seen better on the scan.

Receiving MRI scans on a regular basis is important for monitoring the growth of tumours and for detecting the development of any new ones.

Living with NF2

NF2 is a very serious disease. The people who have it, their families and their doctor (GP) need to deal with all of its implications. People with NF2 have to monitor their body closely and they have to be watched closely by those around them.

Only in rare cases is it possible to correct neurological damage with surgery once it has occurred.

Deafness or hearing loss is the most common symptom experienced by people with NF2. Vestibular disorders (vertigo) and paralysis in the arms or legs can also occur, which can lead to walking disabilities. Most of the people affected by NF2 also suffer from a loss of vision.

People with NF2 have to expect that they will suffer from severe hearing loss or will lose their hearing completely. Even if a patient's operation for preserving their hearing is initially successful, it doesn't necessarily mean that they will be able to hear for the rest of their lives because acoustic neuromas frequently reoccur in patients with NF2 (relapse). For most people with NF2, hearing loss is the symptom that most seriously disrupts a person's plans for their life. But nobody with NF2 is alone. For many, talking to others with the disease is an essential step in learning how to cope with its challenges. Thankfully there is a national support group for people with NF2 in Germany that can provide assistance.

This self-help group is organised by people who have NF2, it is very active, and it keeps people updated regularly through email and a discussion forum. The group holds annual meetings and seminars where people with NF2 can get useful tips on how to deal with the different problems they are facing in their everyday, work and family lives which develop as a result of operations and disabilities.

Technical devices for deaf patients
In addition to hearing aids for people who have hearing loss, there are also new ways for people who have become comple-

tely deaf to regain their hearing, namely cochlear implants and brain stem implants. The way in which these devices function has significantly improved over the past few years and implants have become suitable options for many people who are deaf.

Cochlear implants (CI) are devices that stimulate the auditory pathway with electrical impulses in patients who are either profoundly or totally deaf. Cochlear implants have two components comprising of an implant that is placed under the skin behind the ear during surgery and an external speech processor, which is worn by the patient like a small hearing aid. The speech processor can be removed whenever the patient wants and it works without any external plug connectors. A prerequisite for using a CI is that the auditory nerve still has to function properly.

People who are deaf due to NF2 often have auditory nerves that have been severely damaged, although there are cases where the auditory nerve in the inner ear is still intact. In these cases, a CI can be usually be used. In terms of results, cochlear implants are considerably superior to brain stem implants. Auditory nerves can be examined by specialists in an ENT (ears, nose and throat) hospital to determine whether they function well enough for using a CI.

Auditory brain stem implants (ABI) are used in patients whose auditory nerves no longer function. People with NF2 require this type of implant more often than a CI. The implants are usually put into place at the same time vestibular schwannomas are removed. For the most part, the technology behind the brain stem implant is similar to the technology used in cochlear implants. However one difference is that in an ABI the electrodes are connected to the brain stem so that they can stimulate the brain stem, which is responsible for the auditory pathway.

Great advancements have been made in the past few years for both types of implants. In its early developmental stages an ABI was significantly inferior to a CI and it only enabled patients to perceive sounds; however ABIs have improved so much that today it is possible for people with these implants to understand language under good acoustic and lighting conditions, although, its benefits can vary greatly from person to person. In some cases people with brain stem implants can even talk on the telephone (primarily with people who they know well).

Even with cochlear and brain stem implants serious hearing impairment is still common. It is for this reason that many people with NF2 learn sign language. Sign language makes it possible for them to express themselves and communicate fluently, regardless of their hearing status or the technical aids they are using.

Frequently asked questions about Neurofibromatosis type 2

How likely is it for a child to develop NF2 if his mother or father has the disease, or if two siblings and a parent have the disease?

The likelihood that a child gets NF2 if a parent has NF2 is 50%, regardless of the child's gender and regardless of whether there are other family members who have the disease.

Do all people with NF2 become deaf? When people with NF2 lose their hearing, do they lose it suddenly or does the hearing loss progress slowly over time?

Today, many people with NF2 still become totally deaf but some retain some of their hearing, often only on one side. Hearing loss can occur gradually over several months or years, it can also occur suddenly from one day to the next or it can happen progressively over the course of a week. It is also common for so-called sudden acute hearing loss to occur. Moreover, deafness is often the result of the surgical interventions to remove a tumour from the auditory nerve.

Are NF1 and NF2 related?

No. Neurofibroma type 1 and 2 are two different genetic disorders that have different causes and effects. In the past, doctors mistakenly considered them as two forms of the same disease known as 'von Recklinghausen disease'.

How are NF2 tumours different from cancer?

A distinction is generally made between benign and malignant tumours. Generally speaking, NF2 tumours are benign tumours because unlike cancerous tumours, they grow slowly and do not spread to other parts of the body. In other words, they do not lead to malignant growths in other sites of the body (metastasis). The likelihood that cancerous tumours will develop out of NF2 tumours is very low.

Can NF2 ever be cured?

Today there is still no cure for NF2. A future cure depends on advancements in science.

Does having NF2, mean that I will die from the disease at a young age?

Previous studies have shown that the average life expectancy of a person with NF2 is considerably shorter than the average life expectancy for the general population. However, life expectancy has increased significantly for people with NF2 as a result of improvements in the diagnostic methods and the monitoring capabilities available and in the surgical methods currently being used. The extent to which

NF2 influences a person's life expectancy depends on the severity of the disease's progression. There are cases where NF2 does not have any impact on life expectancy, conversely there are also cases where NF2 has led to death at a relatively young age.

If I lose my hearing because of NF2, can I still lead a normal life, go to work and drive a car?

No one can imagine what it is really like to be deaf until they actually become deaf. It has a profound effect on every aspect of a person's life. People with NF2 more or less have to reorganise their lives depending on their personality, social contacts, level of education and professional status. But once they have gone through the painful process of coming to terms with their new situation, they can enjoy the wonderful things in life, just like other people. It is possible for people with NF2 to live a normal life, including working. However, it does take a lot of effort. They will have to make adjustments to their lives and make special arrangements for their particular circumstances.

Being able to work depends on a number of factors. In principle, there are a variety of different options available for integrating people with disabilities in the workforce which are being promoted by the special integration service providers and the Integration Office in Germany.

It is also possible for people with hearing loss to drive a car. However if they are completely deaf, driving requires more concentration, since they will not be able to recognise acoustic warning signals like honking or sirens from ambulances.

(The information about NF2 is taken from the German brochure 'Information on Neurofibromatosistosis Type 2', which is published by the German NF2 Self-help Group.)

How this book came to be

I did not write this book by myself. My special thanks goes to the people who have been with me during the past twelve years and above all to those who have supported me with the realisation of this book. Goldi should be mentioned here and others who at the time of my blog kept shouting, "Hey man, you've got to write a book!" I also wanted my poems to be made public, providing there were enough of them.

I started the book in Catalonia in 2014. At first I wrote in English and then I switched to German, I realised that more things came to mind that way. Prior to that, I took my English poems to Barcelona and tried to translate them. Man, that was hard work!

Renate Blaes, my publisher in Germany, played a central role in ensuring that this book saw the light of day. Her publishing house supported me with my many questions and issues. My friend René shot the cover photo in Cuba and wrote the blurb. Then there's Brigitte who supported me in all aspects of life with her wisdom and her advice.

As for the English translation: Firstly, I am sorry that I did not manage to finish this earlier than two years later the German version was published. Amongst other things, NF2 and a very long recovery phase hindered with this. But better late than never, right? I realised that translating, editing and proof-reading a book is much more of a project than I thought it would be. Generally, I find, that the process of translation is so much underestimated. I would have never managed this by myself without the help of the four native English speakers, angels more like, which are mentioned on the first page. Together, they have managed to transform this book into beautiful English language. And then there's Paul; who volunteered to help me, to hunt down the undesirable typo demon and awkward phrases. Basically a final proof-read to polish things up. And of course Jess and Can you hear us, where this book is available for purchase.

And last but not least there's my family; this is simply because they exist and because they carry me through thick and thin.

Unsuccessful book titles:
– Happy-sad
– For me every day is wonderful
– Moment
– 99 per cent
– When up hill means down dale
– Win-win
– The same but different

One Pound of every copy sold will be donated to the NF2 UK self-help group 'Can your hear us!', which enables NF2ers in the UK, including myself!